¡Es muy fácil!

Spanish for Law Enforcement Personnel

Shawn Redwood

Order this book online at www.trafford.com
or email orders@trafford.com

Most Trafford titles are also available at major online book retailers.

Printed in Victoria, BC, Canada.

ISBN: 978-1-4269-3168-0

Library of Congress Control Number:

*Our mission is to efficiently provide the world's finest, most comprehensive book publishing
service, enabling every author to experience success. To find out how to publish your book, your
way, and have it available worldwide, visit us online at www.trafford.com*

Trafford rev. 04/13/2010

 www.trafford.com

North America & international
toll-free: 1 888 232 4444 (USA & Canada)
phone: 250 383 6864 ♦ fax: 812 355 4082

Scope and Sequence

CONTINUED . . .

Un poco de todo 2 65   Las palabras interrogativas

Preface

Why a book such as this one?

Welcome to Spanish for Law Enforcement Personnel, as text designed for beginning level langauge students who are currently working or who will be working in law enforcement. There has been a rapid increase in the number of Spanish-speakers, both legal and illegal, in the United States. This has a tremendous impact on American society, but nowhere else is this impact felt more than on law enforcement agencies. Departments are struggling to meet the needs of Spanish-speakers with very little English-speaking abilities. Language and cultural barriers interfere with basic communication and can prevent an officer from doing his job effectively.

How will this book help me to learn Spanish?

This text is different from others in the field, for it does not assume that you already know Spanish. You learn *need to know* phrases and grammar, which are minimized and presented as an effective means of communication. You will be taught how to participate in everyday conversations with Spanish-speakers, while at the same time be guided through a variety of work related activities. There will be ample opportunity for you to use Spanish in real-life situations. You will spend class time doing communicative activities that use the basic vocabulary essential to the field of law enforcement.

What are some of the way that I can effectively learn Spanish?

Learning another language does not have to be a stressful experience. Here are some tips to get you started. Listen to the language first and allow it to come to you naturally. Seek opportunities to practice your newly acquired language skills with native Spanish-speakers.

One of the most enjoyable ways to use or learn Spanish is to watch movies or listen to the radio in another language. Don't try to undertsand every word, but rather listen to the language in order to train your ear. You will hear Spanish at a natural pace. Don't become frustrated. Watch at least 10 minutes of a film in Spanish everyday. Although learning a language is work, the efforts will pay off quickly when you finally get to use Spanish.

On index cards, copy down words, phrases and expressions that you need right away. You can also cut out the vocabulary cards found in the appendix. Carry them around as a reference tool. Study these cards when you have down time on the job or some extra time to yourself. Follow these guidelines everyday and watch as your language abilities soar.

A Guide to
¡Es muy fácil!: Spanish for Law Enforcement Personnel

Chapter opening page

Each chapter begins with an organizing outline of what each chapter contains: thematic vocabulary, grammar and pronunciation.

Introduction

Introduces a theme relating to a situation that is likely to be encountered by law enforcement personnel.

In this chapter

Presents vocabulary and grammar points taught within each chapter that relate to the chapter theme.

¡Así lo decimos!

The core vocabulary of each chapter is presented in easy to reference Spanish-English lists.

Nota gramatical

Eases you into grammar with definitions of grammatical terms. This section also summarizes grammar points in a simple and accessible way. Explanations have been written to be precise so that you won't get lost in a lengthy discussion.

Práctica - Conversación

Immediately follow the presentation of vocabulary and grammar points. This is your first step to practice vocabulary and grammar in a situational context.

Just for fun

Gives you a chance to practice what you have learned in a fun and energizing way.

¡Así lo pronunciamos!

Teaches you how to pronounce sounds in Spanish correctly. This section compares both Spanish and English pronunciations.

Un poco de todo

Appears after every chapter. It features relevant cultural aspects of the Spanish-speaking world, a new grammatical concept and a review that integrates vocabulary and grammar from the previous chapter.

Vocabulario útil

Presents vocabulary that is essential to that chapter. You should make an effort to familiarize yourself with the words or expressions that are presented in this section.

ABOUT THE AUTHOR

Shawn Redwood graduated from Virginia Commonwealth University in 1997 with a BA in Spanish and a minor in French. As an undergraduate, he studied in Guatemala, Costa Rica and Puerto Rico. He returned to the University of Puerto Rico in 1998 to do graduate work in linguistics. He received his MA in Spanish from Middlebury College in 2003. The majority of his degree work was completed in Madrid, Spain. He returned to Madrid to teach English in many well-known international companies (2003 – 2006). He also did a full-time internship position as Program Officer Assistant at the Fulbright Commission Spain.

In 2007, Shawn was awarded a grant through The Department of Education of the Madrid Regional Government to be a North American Language and Culture Assistant at Federico García Lorca, a bilingual public school in the north of Madrid. He is currently an English Language Assistant at the charter school Colegio Espíritu Santo in Madrid and is a Teacher Trainer at the Rey Juan Carlos University.

Shawn's principal areas of interest and research are bilingual and international education, Spanish language and linguistics and teaching specialized Spanish classes to adult learners. He has taught Spanish for Law Enforcement and Emergency Personnel both at J. Sargeant Reynolds Community College and at the Richmond Police Training Academy.

Introduction

This chapter will give you the skills and practice necessary to speak Spanish with confidence. Learning a foreign language takes time. With a lot of practice and patience, you will become successful in getting your point across and in being understood by native Spanish-speakers.

In This Chapter

COMUNICACIÓN

- ☑ **Greetings and farewells**
- ☑ **Days of the week**
- ☑ **Months of the year**
- ☑ **Personal information**
- ☑ **Asking for repetition**

ESTRUCTURAS

- ☑ **Numbers 0-100**
- ☑ **Telling time**

PRONUNCIACIÓN

- ☑ **The Spanish alphabet**
- ☑ **Spanish vowels**
- ☑ **B, V, P**
- ☑ **C, S, X, Z**

1. The Basics

1. Hola. ¿Cómo está Ud.?

¡Así lo decimos!

✖ **GREETINGS**

Hola.	*Hello.*
Buenos días.	*Good morning.*
Buenas tardes.	*Good afternoon.*
Buenas noches.	*Good evening.*

✖ **ASKING HOW A PERSON IS DOING**

¿Cómo está Ud.?[1]	
¿Cómo estás (tú)?[2]	*How are you?*

Muy bien, gracias.	*Very well, thanks.*
Bien.	*Fine.*

Así, así.	
Más o menos.	*OK.*
Regular.	

Mal.	*Bad.*
Muy mal.	*Very bad.*

✖ **EXPRESSIONS OF COURTESY**

Por favor.	*Please.*
Gracias.	*Thank you.*

De nada.	
No hay de qué.	*You're welcome.*
Por nada.	

✖ **FAREWELLS**

Adiós.	*Good-bye.*
Hasta pronto.	*See you soon.*
Hasta luego.	*See you later.*
Hasta mañana.	*See you tomorrow.*

---

[1] **Usted** is the formal, singular form of *you*. It is used to address a person you do not know well or a person to whom you would show respect. **Usted** is generally abbreviated **Ud.**

[2] **Tú** is the familiar, singular form of *you*. It is used to address a person you would call by a first name, such as a relative, friend or child. The **tú** is often omitted in speech.

✖ **ASKING SOMEONE'S NAME**

¿Cóme se llama Ud.?
¿Cómo te llamas? } *What's your name?*

Me llamo . . . *My name is . . .*

✖ **TITLES**

señor (Sr.) *Mr., sir*
señora (Sra.) *Mrs., ma'am*
señorita (Srta.) *Miss (There is no Spanish equivalent for Ms.)*

✖ **OTHER USEFUL EXPRESSIONS:**

por favor. *please.*
   (also used to get someone's attention)

perdón. *pardon me, excuse me*
   (to ask forgiveness or to get someone's attention)

con permiso. *pardon me, excuse me*
   (to ask permission to pass through a group of people)

Conversación

A. **Cortesía**. How would you respond to the each greeting or phrase below?

1. Buenas tardes. _____

2. Adiós. _____

3. Hola. _____

4. ¿Cómo está Ud.? _____

5. Buenas noches. _____

6. Muchas gracias. _____

7. Hasta mañana. _____

8. ¿Cómo se llama Ud.? _____

9. Buenos días. _____

B. **Situaciones**. How would you greet the following people in Spanish?

1. Mrs. María Garcia, 8:00 A.M.   _____

2. Mr. José Soto, 3:15 P.M.   _____

3. Miss Amanda Murphy, 9:30 P.M.   _____

4. Ms. Lupe Gómez, 5:00 P.M.   _____

5. Mr. Ramón Carrasco, 11:15 A.M.   _____

C. **Entrevista**. Turn to the person sitting next to you and do the following:

- Greet him or her appropriately (informal forms)
- Find out his or her name.
- Ask how he or she is.
- Say good-bye.

2. El alfabeto español

Study the Spanish alphabet below. Note that the letter **rr** is a separate letter and represents a single sound.

Letra	Nombre	Ejemplo
a	a	ambulancia
b	be	bomba
c	ce	cara
ch*	che	chimenea
d	de	doctor
e	e	emergencia
f	efe	falso
g	ge	gasolina
h	hache	herida
i	i	identificar
j	jota	jeringa
k	ka	kilo
l	ele	legal
ll*	elle	llama
m	eme	medicina

¡Así lo decimos!

n	ene	narcóticos
ñ	eñe	señor
o	o	oxígeno
p	pe	paciente
q	cu	queja
r	ere	robo
rr	erre	carro
s	ese	seguro
t	te	terremoto
u	u	urgente
v	uve	víctima
w	doble uve	Washington
x	equis	examinar
y	i griega (ye)	yeso
z	zeta	zanja

In 1994, the Royal Spanish Language Academy declared that **ch** and **ll** are no longer letters of the Spanish alphabet. These two letters are included in our list because you may hear some of the Hispanics that you encounter use **ch** and **ll** when they spell their names. The letters **k** and **w** appear only in words borrowed from other languages. To distinguish between the letters **b** and **v** in spelling, you will hear many Spanish-speakers say **b (be grande)** and **v (be chica)**.

Práctica

A. How well do you know the Spanish alphabet?

1. These letters are not found in the English alphabet.
2. This letter is never pronounced.
3. These two letters appear only in words borrowed from other languages.
4. These two letters are no longer a part of the Spanish alphabet.

B. **¿Qué palabra es?** Your instructor will spell 5 words. Write down each word that you hear. Be ready to read your word in class.

1. _____

2. _____

3. _____

4. _____

5. _____

Conversación

A. **Tu nombre, por favor**. Spell your own name in Spanish aloud, and listen as your classmates spell their names. Try to remember as many names as you can.

B. **Los Estados Unidos**. You know more Spanish than you think. The names of many U.S. cities and states are of Hispanic origin. Pronounce the names in Spanish of each U.S. city or state below. Then, spell it aloud in Spanish.

NEVADA   COLORADO   AMARILLO   EL PASO   FLORIDA   LAS VEGAS

C. **¿Puede deletrear su nombre?** You have just pulled over 5 people in a car for running a red light. They are Cuban and speak very little English. Ask them to spell their name. Working with a partner, one will play the part of the police officer and the other person will be one of the Cuban passengers.

Policía: ¿Cómo se llama Ud.?

Pasajero: Me llamo Jorge Morales.

Policía: ¿Puede deletrear su nombre, por favor?

Pasajero: Sí. Mi nombre es jota-o-ere-ge-e. Mi apellido es eme-o-ere-a-ele-e-ese.

Policía: Gracias.

Pasajero: De nada.

1. María Vaca
2. Andrés Plata
3. Javier Gonzáles
4. Miguel Martín
5. Elena Santillana

> **Nota Lexical**
>
> Another way to get a person to spell their name is to ask, **¿Cómo se escribe su nombre?**.

3. Los números 0 a 100

1 2 3 . . .

Numbers are used to get a person's address, age, height, license plate, telephone or social security number. Learning numbers in Spanish will help you to obtain a person's vital information.

¡Así lo decimos!

0	**cero**	15	**quince**	30	**treinta**
1	**uno**	16	**dieciséis**	31	**treinta y uno**
2	**dos**	17	**diecisiete**	40	**cuarenta**
3	**tres**	18	**dieciocho**	42	**cuarenta y dos**
4	**cuatro**	19	**diecinueve**	50	**cincuenta**
5	**cinco**	20	**veinte**	53	**cincuenta y tres**
6	**seis**	21	**veintiuno**	60	**sesenta**
7	**siete**	22	**veintidós**	64	**sesenta y cuatro**
8	**ocho**	23	**veintitrés**	70	**setenta**
9	**nueve**	24	**veinticuatro**	75	**setenta y cinco**
10	**diez**	25	**veinticinco**	80	**ochenta**
11	**once**	26	**veintiséis**	86	**ochenta y seis**
12	**doce**	27	**veintisiete**	90	**noventa**
13	**trece**	28	**veintiocho**	99	**noventa y nueve**
14	**catorce**	29	**veintinueve**	100	**cien**

Nota gramatical

UNO, HAY, ¿CUÁNTOS?

✖ **Uno** shortens to **un** before a masculine noun. Before feminine nouns, **uno** changes to **una**. *Chapter 2 will explain more about nouns and gender*.

veintiún hombres	*21 men*
cincuenta y una mujeres	*51 women*

✖ **Hay** means *there is* or *there are*.

Hay un carro en el garaje.	*There is a car in the garage.*
Hay diecinueve pistolas.	*There are 19 pistols.*

✖ To ask *How many?* use **¿Cuántos?** before masculine nouns and **¿Cuántas?** before feminine nouns.

¿Cuántos sospechosos hay?	*How many suspects are there?*
¿Cuántas personas hay?	*How many people are there?*

✖ To ask for a person's telephone number say **¿Cuál es su número de teléfono?** Many Spanish-speakers say telephone numbers in the following way: 7 59 83 37 (*siete-cincuenta y nueve-ochenta y tres-treinta y siete*). Some Spanish-speakers use single digits.

Práctica

A. **¿Qué número es?** Write down the number that you hear your instructor say in Spanish.

1. _____   2. _____   3. _____   4. _____   5. _____

B. Read the following numbers aloud in Spanish.

1. 87   2. 99   3. 21   4. 75   5. 15

Conversación

Entrevista. How many are there of each person or item?

1. ¿Cuántos sospechosos hay en la cárcel? **25**
2. ¿Cuántas pistolas hay aquí? **57**
3. ¿Cuántos carros hay en el garaje? **61**
4. ¿Cuántas mujeres hay en el departamento? **83**
5. ¿Cuantas bombas hay en la casa? **3**

¡Así lo pronunciamos!

LAS VOCALES

Spanish vowels are never silent. They are pronounced in a short, crisp way without the glide sounds used in English.

| a | The Spanish **a** closely resembles the English *a* in the word *father*. |

ALTO   CASA   MAYO   BANANA   ANTES

| e | The Spanish **e** is pronounced like the English e word *eight*. |

EL   ENERO   LECHE   COMER   ENTRE

| i | The Spanish **i** is pronounced like *ee* as in the English word *see*. |

IGLESIA   IGNACIO   INOCENTE   LINDA   HILO

| o | The Spanish **o** has the same pronunciation as the English *o* in *obey*. |

OLOR   ORINA   OFICINA   OCHENTA   MALO

| u | The Spanish **u** has the same pronunciation as the English *oo* in *soon*. |

USAR   LUNES   ÚLTIMO   UNO   JURADO

4. La hora

08:25

To ask what time it is in Spanish you can say **¿Qué hora es?** or **¿Qué horas son?**.

Es la una.	*It's one o'clock.*
Son las dos.	*It's two o'clock.*
Son las tres.	*It's three o'clock.*

Do you see a pattern? Continue telling time in Spanish.

✖ Use **y** to tell time until half past.

Son las tres y diez.	*It's 3:10.*
Son las seis y cuarto[1].	*It's 6:15.*
Son las siete y media[2].	*It's 7:30.*

✖ Use **menos** when the minutes go past thirty.

Son las dos menos veinte[3].	*It's 1:40.*
Son las nueve menos cuarto.	*It's 8:45.*
Son las once menos diez.	*It's 10:50.*

✖ To express **noon** and **midnight**:

Es mediodía	*It's noon.*
Es medianoche.	*It's midnight.*

---

1. **Quince** is also used.
2. **Treinta** is also used.
3. *It is two o'clock minus twenty.*

¡Así lo decimos!

Práctica

A. **¡Atención!** Listen as your instructor says a time of day. Find the time that corresponds to the time you heard and say its letter in Spanish.

PARA EXPRESAR LA HORA

✓ When a specific time is expressed, use:

de la mañana	*in the morning*
de la tarde	*in the afternoon*
de la noche	*in the evening*

Son las tres y diez de la tarde.
   It's 3:10 in the afternoon.

✓ When a specific time is not expressed, use:

por la mañana	*in the morning*
por la tarde	*in the afternoon*
por la noche	*in the evening*

Elena estudia por la noche.
   Elena studies in the evening.

✓ To ask at what time an event will occur, say **¿A qué hora es?**.

¿A qué hora es la fiesta?
   At what time is the party?

✓ Use the preposition **a** to express *at*.

Es a las tres de la tarde.
   It's at 3:00 in the afternoon.

✓ To express *exactly*, *on the dot* or *sharp*, use **en punto**.

Son las dos de la tarde en punto.
   It's exactly 2:00 P.M.

a. 11:40   c. 2:00   e. 10:23   g. 2:20

b. 5:15   d. 9:30   f. 1:05   h. 6:18

B. **¿Qué hora es?** Read each of the times below in Spanish.

1. 1:00   3. 11:00   5. 3:15   7. 10:40

2. 6:00   4. 1:30   6. 6:45   8. 2:50

C. **Relojes**. Write the times below on each digital clock.

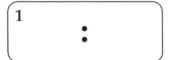
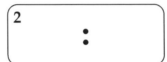
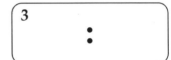

1. Son las nueve y media.
2. Son las ocho menos cuarto.
3. Es la una y diez.
4. Son las cuatro menos cinco.
5. Son las doce en punto.

Conversación

Entervista. Ask a classmate at what time the following activities take place.

1. ¿A qué hora es el entrenamiento? **3:45**
2. ¿A qué hora es el juicio? **9:00**
3. ¿A qué hora es la ceremonia? **11:30**
4. ¿A qué hora es la audencia? **2:15**
5. ¿A qué hora es la clase de español? **5:00**

¡Así lo pronunciamos!

B, V, P

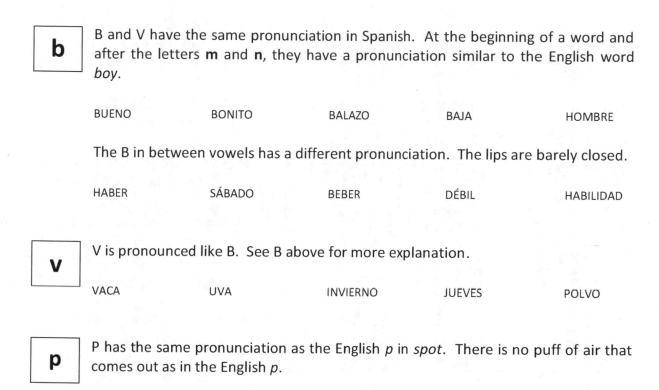

b | B and V have the same pronunciation in Spanish. At the beginning of a word and after the letters **m** and **n**, they have a pronunciation similar to the English word *boy*.

BUENO   BONITO   BALAZO   BAJA   HOMBRE

The B in between vowels has a different pronunciation. The lips are barely closed.

HABER   SÁBADO   BEBER   DÉBIL   HABILIDAD

v | V is pronounced like B. See B above for more explanation.

VACA   UVA   INVIERNO   JUEVES   POLVO

p | P has the same pronunciation as the English *p* in *spot*. There is no puff of air that comes out as in the English *p*.

PAPEL   PERO   PARA   PUERTA   PITAR

5. El calendario

25 de marzo

¡Así lo decimos!

ENERO	FEBRERO	MARZO
L M M J V S D	L M M J V S D	L M M J V S D
1 2 3 4 5 6 7	1 2 3 4	1 2 3 4
8 9 10 11 12 13 14	5 6 7 8 9 10 11	5 6 7 8 9 10 11
15 16 17 18 19 20 21	12 13 14 15 16 17 18	12 13 14 15 16 17 18
22 23 24 25 26 27 28	19 20 21 22 23 24 25	19 20 21 22 23 24 25
29 30 31	26 27 28	26 27 28 29 30 31

ABRIL	MAYO	JUNIO
L M M J V S D	L M M J V S D	L M M J V S D
1	1 2 3 4 5 6	1 2 3
2 3 4 5 6 7 8	7 8 9 10 11 12 13	4 5 6 7 8 9 10
9 10 11 12 13 14 15	14 15 16 17 18 19 20	11 12 13 14 15 16 17
16 17 18 19 20 21 22	21 22 23 24 25 26 27	18 19 20 21 22 23 24
23/30 24 25 26 27 28 29	28 29 30 31	25 26 27 28 29 30

JULIO	AGOSTO	SEPTIEMBRE
L M M J V S D	L M M J V S D	L M M J V S D
1	1 2 3 4 5	1 2
2 3 4 5 6 7 8	6 7 8 9 10 11 12	3 4 5 6 7 8 9
9 10 11 12 13 14 15	13 14 15 16 17 18 19	10 11 12 13 14 15 16
16 17 18 19 20 21 22	20 21 22 23 24 25 26	17 18 19 20 21 22 23
23/30 24/31 25 26 27 28 29	27 28 29 30 31	24 25 26 27 28 29 30

OCTUBRE	NOVIEMBRE	DICIEMBRE
L M M J V S D	L M M J V S D	L M M J V S D
1 2 3 4 5 6 7	1 2 3 4	1 2
8 9 10 11 12 13 14	5 6 7 8 9 10 11	3 4 5 6 7 8 9
15 16 17 18 19 20 21	12 13 14 15 16 17 18	10 11 12 13 14 15 16
22 23 24 25 26 27 28	19 20 21 22 23 24 25	17 18 19 20 21 22 23
29 30 31	26 27 28 29 30	24/31 25 26 27 28 29 30

LOS DÍAS DE LA SEMANA

lunes	*Monday*
martes	*Tuesday*
miércoles	*Wednesday*
jueves	*Thursday*
viernes	*Friday*
sábado	*Saturday*
domingo	*Sunday*

LOS MESES DEL AÑO

enero	*January*
febrero	*February*
marzo	*March*
abril	*April*
mayo	*May*
junio	*June*
julio	*July*
agosto	*August*
septiembre	*September*
octubre	*October*
noviembre	*November*
diciembre	*December*

PARA EXPRESAR LA FECHA

✖ The Spanish calendar starts with **Monday**.

✖ Days of the week and months of the year are not capitalized in Spanish.

✖ To ask for today's date, say **¿Cuál es la fecha de hoy?**.

✖ You would respond by saying, **Hoy es el tres de julio**, for example.

✖ There are several ways to write the date in Spanish. To express July 9, 2002 in Spanish, you can write: **9 de julio de (del) 2002** or **9-7-2002**.

✖ When July 9, 2002 is written as 9-7-2002, it can be misleading. To avoid this, Spanish-speakers write the month using a Roman numeral: **9-VII-2002**.

Expresiones de tiempo

el día	*day*
la semana	*week*
el mes	*month*
el año	*year*
mañana	*tomorrow*
ayer	*yesterday*

Práctica

A. **Los días de la semana**. Using the calendar on page 13, indicate the day of the week on which the following dates fall.

1. 2 de mayo   _____

2. 21 de diciembre   _____

3. 8 de enero   _____

4. 3 de junio   _____

5. 16 de agosto   _____

6. 27 de marzo   _____

7. 1 de septiembre   _____

B. **La fecha**. Write each of the dates below in Spanish.

1. July 23, 1994

   _____

2. November 24, 1868

   _____

3. February 14, 2002

   _____

4. October 31, 1973

   _____

5. April 1, 1776

   _____

Conversación

Preguntas. Answer each question below.

1. ¿Cuántos días hay en una semana?
2. ¿Cuántos días hay en un fin de semana (*weekend*)?
3. ¿Cuántos días hay en un mes?
4. ¿Cuantos meses hay en un año?
5. ¿Qué día es hoy?
6. ¿Qué día es mañana?
7. Si hoy es lunes, ¿qué día es mañana?
8. Si hoy es viernes, ¿qué día es mañana?
9. ¿Qué día fue (*was*) ayer?
10. ¿Qué días de la semana no tenemos (*don't we have*) clase?

¡Así lo pronunciamos!

C, S, X, Z

C	C has two sounds in Spanish. When it is before **a**, **o**, **u**, **l** or **r** it has a *k* sound, as in the English word *count*.

CARO	CASO	CULPABLE	CALVO	CAJA

Before the letters **i** and **e**, C has the *s* sound as in the English word *see*.

CELDA	CERO	CINTURÓN	COCHE	CENTAVO

S	S has the same pronunciation as the English *s* in *see*.

SITIO	SOLO	SALIR	SUCIO	BASTANTE

When it comes before **d** and **m**, it has a sound comparable to *z*, but not as hard.

DESDE	MISMO

CONTINUED . . .

X	X has a pronunciation like the combination GS.

EXACTO   EXAMINAR   EXAGERAR

Before a consonant, X is pronounced like the English S

EXPERTO   EXTRANJERO   EXTENDER

Z	Z has the *s* sound as in the English word *see*.

ZAPATO   ZANJA   COMENZAR   ZURDO   VEZ

La información personal

Vocabulario útil

✖ **NAME**

¿Cómo se llama Ud.?	*What's your name?*
¿Cuál es su nombre?	
Nombre.	*Name.*

Soy . . .	*I'm . . .*
Me llamo . . .	*I'm called . . .*
Mi nombre es . . .	*My name is . . .*

TO GET A PERSON'S FULL, LEGAL NAME

Nombre de pila	*First name*
Segundo nombre	*Middle name*
Apellido	*Last name*

✖ **AGE**

¿Cuántos años tiene?	*How old are you?*
¿Qué edad tiene?	
¿Cuál es su edad?	
Edad.	*Age.*

> In many Spanish-speaking countries, on all official documents, persons are given two last names. Take the example of **Juan Miguel Ruiz González**. The first last name (**Ruiz**) is that of Juan's father; the second (**González**) is that of his mother's. This system is not widely used by Hispanics living in this country.

✖ **ADDRESS**

¿Cuál es su dirección?	*What is your address?*
¿Dónde vive Ud.?	*Where do you live?*
Dirección.	*Address.*

✖ **MARITAL STATUS**

¿Cuál es su estado civil?	*What is your marital status?*
Estado civil.	*Marital status.*

soltero(a)	*single*
casado(a)	*married*
divorciado(a)	*divorced*
separado(a)	*separated*
viudo(a)	*widowed*

CONTINUED . . .

✖ SOCIAL SECURITY NUMBER

¿Cuál es su número
     de seguro social?   *What's your social security number?*
Número de seguro social.   *Social security number.*

✖ TELEPHONE NUMBER

¿Cuál es su número
     de teléfono?   *What's your telephone number?*
Número de teléfono.   *Telephone number.*

✖ PLACE OF EMPLOYMENT

¿Dónde trabaja Ud.?   *Where do you work?*
Lugar de trabajo.   *Place of employment.*

Hablo poco español

Here are some simple phrases you can use to ask for repetition or to express a lack of understanding.

Otra vez, por favor. No entiendo.   *Again, please. I don't understand.*

¿Cómo?   *What? I didn't catch that.*

Más despacio, por favor.   *Slower please.*

Repita, por favor. No entendí.   *Repeat, please. I didn't get it.*

Palabra por palabra.   *Word for word.*

Hablo poco español.   *I speak very little Spanish.*

¿Habla Ud. inglés?   *Do you speak English?*

Un poco de todo 1

1. Where in the world is Spanish spoken?

As of 2009, 329 million people speak Spanish as a native language and it is among the top five languages spoken in the world. There are 21 countries that have Spanish as their official language: Spain, North, Central and South America (except Brazil and the Guyanas), the Caribbean (Cuba, Dominican Republic and Puerto Rico) and Africa (Equatorial Guinea). Spanish can also be heard in the Philippines, as well as Andorra, a tiny country that borders Spain and France.

Spanish varies from country to country. The Spanish of Cuba is different from that spoken in Chile or Spain. There are noticeable differences in pronunciation, vocabulary and special expressions, just like in any language. What is called a **papelera** (trash can) in Spain, is called a **zafacón** in Puerto Rico. These differences are noticeable and can *sometimes* result in misunderstandings among native speakers.

> **THINK ABOUT IT**
>
> Is English spoken the same way in the U.S.? How does the English of Great Britain differ from U.S. English? Examples.

MÉXICO, AMÉRICA CENTRAL Y EL CARIBE

MÉXICO

CUBA

REPÚBLICA DOMINICANA

PUERTO RICO

HONDURAS

GUATEMALA

EL SALVADOR

NICARAGUA

COSTA RICA

PANAMÁ

A. **Los países de habla española**. In the following exercise, you will search the Internet to gather information about Spanish-speaking countries. Visit the web site **www.lonelyplanet.com** to answer each question below.

1. How many indigenous languages are spoken in Mexico?

_____.

2. What are the major industries of Argentina?

    _____.

3. How many languages are spoken in Spain?

    _____.

4. Name the two official languages of the Republic of Equatorial Guinea?

    _____.

5. What is the population of Venezuela?

    _____.

6. What percentage of the population of Peru is **mestizo**?

    _____.

7. What religions are practiced in Uruguay?

    _____.

8. What are the major industries of Puerto Rico?

    _____.

9. How many people live in Havana, Cuba?

    _____.

10. What percentage of the population in Ecuador is **Indian**?

    _____.

11. Who is the president of El Salvador?

    _____.

12. Name three of the native languages spoken in Chile.

    _____.

13. What are the major industries of Costa Rica?

_____.

14. Who is the president of the Dominican Republic?

_____.

15. How many Mayan languages are spoken in Guatemala?

_____.

16. What languages are spoken in Nicaragua?

_____.

17. Which countries are major trading partners with Bolivia?

_____.

18. What is the population of Panama?

_____.

19. What type of English is spoken in Honduras?

_____.

20. What is the population of Colombia?

_____.

21. What are the major industries of Paraguay?

_____.

2. Cognates

Many words in Spanish and English are identical or very similar. These words are called **cognates**. Cognates look alike and mean the same or nearly the same thing in both English and Spanish. However, they usually don't sound alike, so at first it will be easier to recognize cognates when you see them than when you hear them. As you become more familiar with Spanish pronunciation, you will recognize spoken cognates more and more easily.

B. **¿Qué es esto?** Can you guess the meaning of each word below?

TIGRE   ESTÉREO   BIOLOGÍA   VOLEIBOL   CONGRESO   GUITARRA   VISITAR

This section will help you to recognize cognates and understand more Spanish. Pay attention to the category to which they belong. Never forget that there are always exceptions to the rule.

ph	All English words that contain the **ph** cluster will have an **f** in Spanish.
	FOTOGRAFÍA TELÉFONO

-ade	English words that end in **–ade** will end in **–ada** in Spanish.
	CASCADA LIMONADA

-ant	English words that end in **–ant** will end in **–ante** in Spanish.
	DISTANTE INSTANTE

-cy	English words that end in **–cy** will end in **–cia** in Spanish.
	DEMOCRACIA INFANCIA

-ty	English words that end in **–ty** will end in **–ad** in Spanish.
	DIVERSIDAD UNIVERSIDAD

CONTINUED . . .

-ic

English words that end in **–ic** will end in **–ica** or **-ico** in Spanish.

PÚBLICO   MÚSICA

-ion

English words that end in **–ion** will end in **–ión** in Spanish.

FUNCIÓN   RELIGIÓN

-ist

English words that end in **–ist** will end in **–ista** in Spanish.

ARTISTA   DENTISTA

s + consonant

All words that begin with **s + consonant** will be preceded by an **e**.

ESCENA   ESPECIALISTA

C. **Los anuncios clasificados**. Read the ads below. Find the Spanish equivalent for the English words.

Centro Dos Caminos, 96 M. cuadrados, tres (3) cubículos, dos (2) baños, tres (3) líneas telefónicas, aire acondicionado central, un (1) puesto de estacionamiento y puestos por hora para visitantes, cuatro (4) ascensores para todos los pisos

---

1. central air   _____

2. visitors   _____

3. telephone lines _____

4. cubicles   _____

5. center   _____

6. parking   _____

> Mínimo 5 años de experiencia en la industria con dos años de experiencia a nivel de operaciones. Con habilidades en el manejo de computadoras preferiblemente completamente bilingüe.

1. computers   _____

2. minimum   _____

3. operations   _____

4. bilingual   _____

5. industry   _____

6. abilities   _____

> Estamos buscando personal motivado que tenga entusiasmo de aprender y deseos de trabajar como parte del equipo que limpia la casa de nuestros clientes. Ofrecemos competitivos salarios y pagamos por entrenamiento profesional, excelentes horarios y oportunidades de ascender. Deben tener experiencia y documentos legales. Después de la segunda semana, garantizamos cuarenta horas.

a. What type of salaries does this company offer?

    _____.

b. What type of people is this company looking for?

    _____.

c. What should a person have before applying for this job?

    _____.

d. What happens after the second week of work?

    _____.

D. **Sopa de letras**. Here are more Spanish cognates that you can add to your vocabulary. Find each word in the puzzle below.

absurdo	arrogante	clase	frecuente	individual	rata
adulto	calendario	crimen	futuro	justicia	tráfico
alfabeto	candidato	documento	humano	motor	uniforme
ambulancia	causa	final	incidente	ofensivo	violento

```
A   R   I   D   Y   L   A   I   P   F   R   J   G   P   C

U   D   A   P   A   B   M   G   U   K   O   F   J   A   E

O   I   U   N   C   R   B   T   H   U   F   R   L   O   T

Y   T   I   L   A   Q   U   M   O   B   E   E   R   D   N

W   F   N   T   T   R   L   T   U   J   N   C   L   R   A

A   I   A   E   O   O   A   X   U   D   S   U   L   U   G

A   Z   M   P   L   D   N   N   A   G   I   E   E   S   O

Y   S   F   G   I   O   C   R   J   F   V   N   O   B   R

L   A   U   D   I   V   I   D   N   I   O   T   T   A   R

L   X   N   A   S   O   A   V   L   A   M   E   E   C   A

N   A   D   O   C   U   M   E   N   T   O   S   B   R   X

C   E   T   N   E   D   I   C   N   I   T   A   A   I   B

J   U   S   T   I   C   I   A   U   N   O   L   F   M   D

E   M   R   O   F   I   N   U   T   U   R   C   L   E   O

T   R   Á   F   I   C   O   N   A   M   U   H   A   N   E
```

3. Los números

E. **Más anuncios**. Which number would you call in each situation? Read your answer aloud.

| Instalación / reparación & restauración de pisos de madera y mantenimiento de todo tipo de piso. Lavado de piso. Lavado y encerado de pisos. Limpieza de alfombras. **642-0857** |

1. The plumbing is bad.

   _____

2. You need to see a dentist.

   _____

| Servicio de mantenimiento para inspección para todo tipo de vehículos. **572-8156** |

3. The car needs a tune up.

   _____

| Plan Médico.   Beneficios, hospitalización,   cuidado dental, cuidado de la vista. **662-4357** |

4. The rugs need cleaning.

   _____

| Servicio de plomería, aire acondicionado, calefacción. **494-1195** |

5. You need to move to a bigger apartment.

   _____

| Ofrecemos los servicios de limpieza y mudanzas.   De apartamentos, Townhouses, casas, oficinas, garajes, áticos. **220-2327** |

6. You need medical insurance.

   _____

4. La hora

F. **¿Qué hora es?** Write the time.

1. Es medianoche.   _____

2. Son las nueve y quince.   _____

3. Son las siete menos cinco.   _____

4. Es la una y media.   _____

5. Son las dos.   _____

6. Son las once menos cuarto.   _____

Just for fun

Sopa de letras. Find the name of 7 countries where Spanish is spoken. Then write the names of these countries in the blanks.

B	K	D	V	R	P	M	S
E	P	A	N	A	M	A	O
L	S	Ñ	U	B	R	I	C
I	P	E	R	U	E	V	I
H	L	I	D	C	N	I	X
C	T	N	O	E	X	L	E
I	O	T	A	N	D	O	M
H	S	D	N	I	O	B	L

1. _____

2. _____

3. _____

4. _____

5. _____

6. _____

7. _____

¡Así lo pronunciamos!

WORD STRESS

Stress can be defined as a syllable receiving a strong relative emphasis. Take a close look at the examples below of stress in Spanish.

1. If a word ends in a **vowel**, **n**, or **s**, stress normally falls on the next to the last syllable.

ca-sa   mo-**chi**-la

2. If the word ends in any other consonant, stress normally falls on the last syllable.

lu-**gar** es-pa-**ñol**

3. Any exceptions to the above rules will have a written accent mark (**un acento ortográfico**) on the stressed vowel.

a-le-**mán** **ó**-pe-ra

Note in particular words that end in -**ía**

dí-a   lo-te-**rí**-a

DIPHTHONGS

A **diphthong** is a combination of a strong vowel (**a**, **e**, **o**) and a weak vowel (**i**, **u**). Both vowels are pronounced as a single syllable. The two weak vowels also form a diphthong. All possible diphthongs in Spanish are listed below.

Stress falls on the first vowel of the diphthong			
ai, ay	caigo, Aragay	**au**	aula
ei, ey	peine, ley	**eu**	neutro
oi, oy	boina, voy	**ou**	boutique

CONTINUED . . .

Stress falls on the second vowel of the diphthong			
ia	hacia	**ie**	viejo
io	dios	**ua**	cuatro
ue	puente	**uo**	cuota

iu *Stress falls on the **u***	viuda	**ui** *Stress falls on the **i***	cuidar

SYLLABICATION

Syllabication is the process of forming or dividing into syllables. Study the rules for syllabication in Spanish. Knowing this will help your pronunciation.

A. Single consonants (including **ch, ll, rr**) are attached to the vowel that follows.

    ca-da   le-che   bo-rra-dor

B. Two consonants are generally separated.

    par-do   i-gual-men-te   es-pa-ñol

C. If a consonant is followed by **l** or **r**, both consonants are attached to the following vowel.

    que-brar   pa-dre   Ga-brie-la

D. The consonant groups **nl, rl, sl, tl, nr** and **sr** are divided.

    Car-los   at-las   En-ri-que

E. The consonant groups **pr, pl, br, bl, fr, fl, tr, dr, cr, cl, gr** and **gl** form a syllable with the vowel that follows.

    a-pro-bar   ca-ble   va-na-glo-ria

CONTINUED . . .

F. Two strong vowels (**a**, **e**, **o**) form separate syllables.

    ca-er   ca-os   le-ón

G. Diphthongs are pronounced as a single syllable.

    E-duar-do   puer-to   es-tu-diar

Práctica

Sílabas. Although all Spanish words of more than one syllable have a stressed vowel, most words do not have a written accent mark. Most words have spoken stress exactly where native speakers of Spanish would predict it. Divide each word below into syllables. Then read them aloud, paying careful attention to where the spoken stress should fall.

1. cuidado   _____

2. lluvia   _____

3. general   _____

4. dólares   _____

5. mujer   _____

6. secretario   _____

7. nueve   _____

8. computadora   _____

9. libertad   _____

10. ochenta   _____

Introduction

This chapter will give you the skills and practice necessary to describe people and name the parts of a car in Spanish. You will also learn vocabulary for clothing and body parts.

In This Chapter

COMUNICACIÓN

- ☑ Body parts
- ☑ Distinguishing features
- ☑ Nationalities
- ☑ Clothing and accessories
- ☑ Colors
- ☑ Car parts

ESTRUCTURAS

- ☑ Articles and nouns
- ☑ Spanish subject pronouns
- ☑ SER
- ☑ TENER
- ☑ Adjectives
- ☑ Regular –ar, –er and –ir verbs
- ☑ Numbers 101 and higher
- ☑ Asking yes / no questions

PRONUNCIACIÓN

- ☑ D, T
- ☑ H, CH
- ☑ LL, Y
- ☑ M, N, Ñ

2. Descriptions

1. Las partes del cuerpo

You must be able to identify the parts of the human body. Memorization and use is the key to learning body parts in Spanish.

¡Así lo decimos!

la cabeza	head	la piel	skin
la frente	forehead	el pelo	hair
el ojo	eye	la ceja	eyelid
la oreja	ear	la nariz	nose
la boca	mouth	los labios	lips
los dientes	teeth	la lengua	tongue
la mejilla	cheek	la mandíbula	cheek
la quijada	jawbone	el mentón	chin
el cuello	neck	el hombro	shoulder
el pecho	chest	el seno	breast
el brazo	arm	el codo	elbow
el antebrazo	forefarm	la mano	hand
el dedo	finger	el pulgar	thumb
el dedo índice	index finger	el dedo del corazón	middle finger
el dedo anular	ring finger	el dedo meñique	little finger
el nudillo	knuckle	la uña	fingernail
la punta del dedo	fingertip	la palma	palm
la muñeca	wrist	el puño	fist
el estómago	stomach	la espalda	back
la cadera	hip	la nalga	buttock
la ingle	groin	el muslo	thigh
la pierna	leg	la rodilla	leg
el tobillo	knee	el pie	
el dedo del pie	toe		

LOS ÓRGANOS VITALES	
el corazón	*heart*
los pulmones	*lungs*
los riñones	*kidneys*
el hígado	*liver*
el intestino delgado	*small intestine*
el intestino gordo	*large intestine*
el apéndice	*appendix*

¿Dónde le duele?

Use this question to ask someone where it hurts. The person will respond with **Me duele(n)** . . . Use **duele** when the body part is singular and **duelen** when it is plural.

Me **duele** el pie.	*My foot hurts.*
Me **duelen** los ojos.	*My eyes hurt.*

Nota gramatical

ARTICLES

✖ An **article** is a word that precedes a noun. There are two types of articles in Spanish: **definite** and **indefinite**. Definite articles express the English word **the**. These articles are listed in the chart below.

	MASCULINE	FEMININE
SINGULAR	**el**	**la**
PLURAL	**los**	**las**

✖ Indefinite articles express the English words **a**, **an**, **some**. These articles are listed in the chart below.

	MASCULINE	FEMININE
SINGULAR	**un**	**una**
PLURAL	**unos**	**unas**

NOUNS

A **noun** is a word that names a person, place, thing, quality, idea or action. Nouns in Spanish, like articles, are either **masculine** or **feminine** and **singular** or **plural**. The article must agree in number and gender with the noun it modifies. The gender for many nouns in Spanish can be determined by the rules that follow.

MASCULINE NOUNS		FEMININE NOUNS	
✖ Refer to males		✖ Refer to females	
el hombre	*man*	la mujer	*woman*
el padre	*father*	la madre	*mother*
✖ End in **–o**		✖ **End in –a**	
el humo	*smoke*	la curita	*bandaid*
el seguro	*insurance*	la navaja	*razor*
✖ End in **–ma**		✖ End in **–ad**	
el problema	*problem*	la enfermedad	*illness*
el síntoma	*symptom*	la mitad	*half*
✖ End in **–men**		✖ End in **–ión**	
el crimen[1]	*crime*	la ración	*ration*
el volumen	*volume*	la televisión	*television*
EXCEPCIONES		**EXCEPCIONES**	
la mano	*hand*	el agua[2]	*water*
la radio	*radio*	el día	*day*
la foto	*photo*	el mapa	*map*
la moto	*motorcycle*	el camión	*truck*

[1] Add an accent in the plural: **crímenes**.

[2] The plural is **las aguas**.

PLURALITY OF NOUNS		
✖ If the noun ends in a vowel, add **–s**.	el carro	**los carros**
✖ If the noun does not end in a vowel, add **–es**.	la ciudad	**las ciudades**
	la nación	**las naciones**[3]
	[3] Drop the accent in the plural.	
✖ If the noun ends in a **–z**, change the **–z** to **–c** before adding **–es**.	la luz	**las luces**

Práctica

A. **¿Qué palabra no pertenece?** Circle the word that doesn't belong.

1.   EL DEDO   LA PALMA   EL PULGAR   EL CUELLO

2.   LA BOCA   LA MUÑECA   LA FRENTE   LA NARIZ

3.   LA PIERNA   LA RODILLA   EL PELO   EL TOBILLO

4.   EL PIE   EL BRAZO   EL HOMBRO   EL CODO

5.   EL CORAZÓN   LOS PULMONES   EL APÉNDICE   LA OREJA

B. **Las asociaciones**. With which part(s) of the body do you associate the following actions? Any verb below that you don't know, consult a Spanish-English dictionary.

    a. tocar   _____

    b. respirar   _____

    c. leer   _____

    d. escuchar   _____

    e. masticar   _____

    f. escribir   _____

    g. probar   _____

    h. patear   _____

    i. sentar   _____

    j. hablar   _____

C. **El mensaje secreto**. Unscramble each of the clue words. Copy the letters in the numbered cells to the other cells with the same number to discover the secret message.

MUÑCEA

NEEDIT

LIEP

ACRA

TEMNÓN

LAAGN

LENGI

DAACER

MOBROH

LEOCUL

D. **El artículo definido**. Write the correct form of the definite article in front of each word below. Afterwards, make both the article and the noun plural.

1. _____ descripción   _____

2. _____ número   _____

3. _____ crimen   _____

4. _____ libertad   _____

5. _____ programa   _____

F. **El artículo indefinido**. Write the correct form of the indefinite article in front of each word below. Afterwards, make both the article and the noun plural.

1. _____ coche   _____

2. _____ luz   _____

3. _____ monumento   _____

4. _____ día   _____

5. _____ caja   _____

Just for fun

¿Dónde le duele? Unscramble the tiles to reveal where it hurts.

_____ .

¡Así lo pronunciamos!

D, T

| d |

D at the beginning of a word and after the letters **l**, **n** and **r** has a pronunciation similar to the English word *David*.

DAGA   FALDA   DÓNDE   TARDE   EL DÍA

The D in between vowels and at the end of a word has a pronunciation which is similar to *th* as in the English word *this*.

CADA   NADA   CUIDADO   USTED   RED

T has the same pronunciation as the English, but the tip of the tongue is placed directly behind the top set of teeth. It is pronounced as the English *t* in the word *stop*.

TALEGA   TÉXAS   TIBIO   TOBILLO   TUBO

2. Los rasgos distintivos

The vocabulary below and the verbs introduced in this section will help you to get a better description of the suspect's face, hair and body features.

DISTINGUISHING FEATURES

el tatuaje	*tattoo*	**el acné**	*acne*
el lunar	*mole*	**las arrugas**	*wrinkles*
la cicatriz	*scar*	**el hoyuelo**	*dimple*
el corte	*cut*	**la verruga**	*wart*
el sarpullido **la erupción**	*rash*	**las pecas**	*freckles*

HAIR

pelo castaño	*brown hair*	**la barba**	*beard*
rubio	*blonde hair*	**la perilla**[1]	*goatee*
corto	*short hair*	**el bigote**	*mustache*
crespo	*curly hair*	**las patillas**	*sideburns*
fino	*fine hair*		
grueso	*thick hair*	[1] also **las barbas de chivo**	
lacio	*straight hair*		
largo	*long hair*		

calvo (a)   *bald*

TEETH

un diente de oro	*gold tooth*	**un diente perdido**	*missing tooth*
un diente de plata	*silver tooth*	**las dentaduras**	*dentures*

¡Así lo decimos!

DESCRIPTIVE ADJECTIVES

ancho (a)	*wide*	**estrecho (a)**	*narrow*
grande	*big*	**pequeño (a)**	*small*
alto (a)	*tall*	**bajo (a)**	*short*
viejo (a)	*old*	**joven**	*young*
bonito (a)	*pretty, attractive*	**feo (a)**	*ugly*
guapo (a)	*good-looking, handsome*		
bueno (a)	*good*	**malo (a)**	*bad*
simpatico (a)	*nice, likeable*	**antipático (a)**	*unpleasant*
delgado (a)	*skinny, thin, slender*	**gordo (a)**	*fat*
flaco (a)			
moreno (a)	*brunette*	**rubio (a)**	*blonde*

ADJECTIVES OF NATIONALITY

argentino (a)	*Argentine*	**hondureño (a)**	*Honduran*
boliviano (a)	*Bolivian*	**mexicano (a)**	*Mexican*
chileno (a)	*Chilean*	**nicaragüense**	*Nicaraguan*
colombiano (a)	*Colombian*	**panameño (a)**	*Panamanian*
costarricense	*Costa Rican*	**paraguayo (a)**	*Paraguayan*
cubano (a)	*Cuban*	**peruano (a)**	*Peruvian*
dominicano (a)	*Dominican*	**puertorriqueño (a)**	*Puerto Rican*
ecuatoriano (a)	*Ecuadorian*	**salvadoreño (a)**	*Salvadoran*
español (a)	*Spanish*	**uruguayo (a)**	*Uruguayan*
guatemalteco (a)	*Guatemalan*	**venezolano (a)**	*Venezuelan*

Nota gramatical

SPANISH SUBJECT PRONOUNS

In order to talk to and about other people, you will need to learn to use subject pronouns in Spanish. These pronouns are listed below. Subject pronouns are not used as frequently in Spanish as they are in English and may usually be omitted.

	SINGULAR		PLURAL	
1st person	**yo**	*I*	**nosotros** **nosotras**	*we*
2nd person	**tú**	*you (familiar)*	**vosotros** **vosotras**	*you (familiar)*
3rd person	**él**	*he*	**ellos**	*they*
	ella	*she*	**ellas**	
	usted	*you (formal)*	**ustedes**	*you (formal)*

In Spanish, there are several ways to say **you**. These words fall into two categories: *familiar* and *formal*.

1. **Tú** is the familiar, singular form of you. It is used to address one person who you would call by a first name, such as a relative, friend or child.

2. **Usted** is the formal, singular form, used to address one person you do not know well or a person to whom you would show respect. It is better to use **usted** when addressing a native speaker; he or she will let you know if it is appropriate to use the **tú** form. **Usted** is generally abbreviated **Ud**.

3. In Latin America and in the United States, **ustedes** is the plural of both **tú** and **usted**. It is used to address two or more persons regardless of your relationship with them. **Ustedes** is generally abbreviated **Uds**.

4. In Spain, **vosotros** and **vosotras** are used as the plural forms of **tú**. **Ustedes** is used only as the plural form of **usted**. You will not learn the **vosotros** form of any verb form in this text.

5. **Nosotras** and **ellas** are used to refer to groups of females. The masculine forms **nosotros** and **ellos** are used for groups of males or for group of both sexes. Even if there is only one male in the group, the masculine form is used.

Práctica

Which subject pronoun would you use to talk about the people below?

1. Gabriel   _____

2. Juan y yo   _____

3. Óscar y Flora   _____

4. Adriana   _____

5. las turistas   _____

6. el chico   _____

7. los conductores   _____

8. el señor y la señora Ruiz _____

SER & TENER

These two verbs will help you to get a better description of a suspect. They are irregular and their forms must be memorized. The verb **SER** has many uses in the Spanish language. A few of them are listed on the next page.

SER (TO BE)			
yo	**soy**	nosotros	**somos**
tú	**eres**		
él		ellos	
ella	**es**	ellas	**son**
Ud.		Uds.	

✖ **Origin**, **possession** & **material**

Soy de Perú.	*I'm from Peru.*
Es el carro de mi abuelo.	*It's my grandfather's car.*
El reloj es de oro.	*The watch is made of gold.*

✖ **Profession**

Pedro es abogado.	*Pedro is a lawyer.*

✖ **Nationality**

Ud. es dominicano.	*You are Dominican.*

✖ **Basic characteristics** (color, size, shape, etc.)

Es alta y muy linda.	*She's tall and very beautiful.*

✖ **Marital status**

Mi tía es divorciada.	*My aunt is divorced.*

✖ **Time** & **date**

Hoy es lunes.	*Today is Monday.*
Son las cinco y media.	*It's 5:30.*

✖ **Events**

La fiesta es en la casa de Juan.	*The party's at Juan's house.*

The Spanish verb **TENER** is used with many words to form common expressions of everyday use in the Spanish language. The English equivalent of the expressions below uses the verb **BE** to express the same idea.

TENER (TO HAVE)	
yo **tengo**	nosotros **tenemos**
tú **tienes**	
él ella **tiene** Ud.	ellos ellas **tienen** Uds.

tener . . .	to be . . .
años	*(so many years) old*
calor	*to be hot*
cuidado	*careful*
frío	*cold*
hambre	*hungry*
miedo	*afraid*
prisa	*in a hurry*
razón	*right*
sed	*thirsty*
sueño	*sleepy*
no tener razón	*to be wrong*

Rogelio siempre tiene prisa.   *Roger is always in a hurry.*

Los niños tienen hambre.   *The children are hungry.*

ADJECTIVES

✖ Adjectives that end in **–o** have four forms.

MORENO	MASCULINE	FEMININE
SINGULAR	**moreno**	**morena**
PLURAL	**morenos**	**morenas**

✖ Adjectives that end in **–e** or in most consonants have only 2 forms: **singular** and **plural**.

GRANDE	MASCULINE	FEMININE
SINGULAR	grande	grande
PLURAL	grandes	grandes

FELIZ	MASCULINE	FEMININE
SINGULAR	feliz	feliz
PLURAL	felices	felices

✖ Most adjectives of nationality have 4 forms.

ESPAÑOL	MASCULINE	FEMININE
SINGULAR	español	española
PLURAL	españoles	españolas

¿Cómo es el sospechoso?

Use this question when you want to get a good description of the suspect. Remember that the adjective must agree with the noun. Look at the examples below.

La nariz es grande.	*His nose is big.*
Los ojos son claros.	*His eyes are clear.*
La frente es muy ancha.	*His forehead is very wide.*
Las orejas son pequeñas.	*His ears are small.*
Él es un poco calvo.	*He's a little bald.*
Tiene un bigote grueso.	*He has a thick mustache.*

Práctica

A. **La descripción.** Go online and find two sketches of criminal suspects. Write a description in Spanish of each suspect and include as much detail as possible. Use the vocabulary on pages 33 – 34 and 40 – 41 and the verbs **ser** and **tener** to help you write your description. Show your pictures to the class.

B. **Las nacionalidades.** Give the nationality of each person below. Use the correct form of the verb **SER**. Remember that the adjective must agree in number and gender with the noun that it modifies. Follow the model.

MODELO   Julio Delgado es de Cuba. *Él es cubano*.

1. María Sánchez es de Puerto Rico.   _____.

2. Yo soy de Guatemala.   _____.

3. Adriana Muñoz es de Nicaragua.   _____.

4. Carla y Maite son de Panamá.   _____.

5. Ricardo y Marta son de Venezuela.   _____.

6. Inés Torres es de Ecuador.   _____.

7. Pilar y yo somos de Bolivia.   _____.

8. Tú eres de Uruguay.   _____.

Just for fun

Write a description of Marge Simpson.

_____

_____

_____

_____

¡Así lo pronunciamos!

H, CH

| h |

H is never pronounced at the beginning of a word in Spanish.

HASTA   HACHE   HUEVO   HÚMEDO   HOLA

| ch |

CH has the same sound as in the English word *change*.

CHALECO   MUCHACHO   CHOCAR   COCHE   CHIMENEA

3. La ropa

This vocabulary will help you to obtain a description of what the suspect was wearing.

CLOTHING & ACCESSORIES

la camisa	shirt	el abrigo	coat
la chaqueta	jacket	el impermeable	raincoat
el suéter	sweater	el reloj	watch
la gorra[1]	baseball cap	el collar	necklace
la blusa	blouse	el brazalete	bracelet
la falda	skirt	la bolsa	purse
la camiseta	t-shirt	las botas	boots
las medias	stocking	la cartera[2]	wallet
el cinturón	belt	las sandalias[3]	sandals
la ropa interior	underwear	el traje	suit
la corbata	tie	el traje de baño	bathing suit
los pantalones	pants	el vestido	dress
los jeans[4]	jeans	los zapatos	shoes
los calcetines	socks	los tenis[5]	tennis shoes

[1] also **la cachucha**
[2] also **la billetera**
[3] also **las chancletas**
[4] also **los vaqueros**
[5] also **los zapatos de tenis**

MATERIAL

de algodón	cotton	de seda	silk
de lana	wool	de poliéster	polyester

STYLE

de cuadros	plaid	de rayas	striped
de lunares	polka-dotted		

¡Así lo decimos!

COLORS

amarillo	yellow	café pardo marrón	brown
anaranjado naranja	orange	rojo	red
azul	blue	rosado	pink
blanco	white	turquesa	turquoise
morado púrpura	purple	violeta	violet
negro	black		

Use **claro** and **oscuro** to distinguish between light and dark colors.

azul claro	light blue	verde oscuro	dark green

Nota gramatical

REGULAR –AR, –ER AND –IR VERBS

In order to communicate effectively, you must learn how to conjugate verbs in Spanish. In this section, you will learn how to conjugate regular –ar, –er and –ir verbs. Study the three model verbs: **llevar**, **correr** and **abrir**.

LLEVAR (TO WEAR, TAKE, CARRY)	
yo llev**o**	nosotros llev**amos**
tú llev**as**	
él ella llev**a** Ud.	ellos ellas llev**an** Uds.

CORRER (TO RUN)	
yo corr**o**	nosotros corr**emos**
tú corr**es**	
él ella corr**e** Ud.	ellos ellas corr**en** Uds.

ABRIR (TO OPEN)	
yo abr**o**	nosotros abr**imos**
tú abr**es**	
él ella abr**e** Ud.	ellos ellas abr**en** Uds.

✖ The endings for −**er** and −**ir** verbs are the same, except for the **nosotros** form.

✖ Some English equivalents to the present tense forms in Spanish are given below.

La mujer **paga** la multa.	*The woman is paying the fine*.
Escribo una carta mañana.	*I'll write a letter tomorrow*.
Ellos **venden** drogas cada día.	*They sell drugs each day*.

✖ The verb **necesitar** is generally followed by a second verb in the infinitive form.

Necesito registrar el carro.	*I need to search the car*.

✖ To make a sentence negative, place **no** before the verb.

Ella **no** paga la multa.	*She isn't paying the fine*.

Práctica

A. **Una descripción detallada.** Your instructor will give you a picture of a person or persons. Give a description of each person in the picture and the clothes that they are wearing. Include as much detail as possible. Use the vocabulary and verbs learned in this section and previous ones.

_____

_____

_____

_____

_____

_____

_____

B. **Los verbos.** Conjugate each verb below in the present tense.

	CAMINAR	COMPRENDER	VIVIR
yo	_____	_____	_____
tú	_____	_____	_____
él ella Ud.	_____	_____	_____
nosotros	_____	_____	_____
ellos ellas Uds.	_____	_____	_____

MÁS PRÁCTICA

Complete verb charts **A – B** in the appendix.

C. **Más verbos**. Complete each sentence with the correct present tense form of the verb in bold print. Then translate the sentences.

1. La policía _____ la puerta. **ABRIR**

   _____.

2. Elena _____ rápido. **MANEJAR**

   _____.

3. Uds. _____ español. **APRENDER**

   _____.

4. Tú _____ una multa. **RECIBIR**

   _____.

5. Los chicos _____ ropa en la calle. **VENDER**

   _____.

6. Mi familia _____ en Chicago. **VIVIR**

   _____.

7. Nosotros _____ al sospechoso. **BUSCAR**

   _____.

8. Los chicos _____ del policía. **CORRER**

   _____.

9. El sospechoso _____ los pantalones azules. **LLEVAR**

   _____.

Asking YES / NO questions

✸ The most common way to form these types of questions is to make your voice rise at the end of the question.

¿Guillermo trabaja aquí?

¿Ud. regresa hoy?

✸ There is always an inverted question mark (¿) at the beginning of a question.

✸ Another way to form a yes / no question is to switch the order of the subject and verb. Your voice still rises at the end of the question.

¿Trabaja Guillermo aquí?

¿Regresa Ud. hoy?

✸ Question tags **¿de acuerdo?**, **¿verdad?** and **¿no?** can also be used. The tag **¿no?** is never used after a negative sentence and ¿de acuerdo? Is used when some kind of action is proposed.

Tú eres chilena, ¿verdad?   You're Chilean, aren't you?

Ud. necesita salir ahora, ¿de acuerdo?   You need to leave now, OK?

Just for fun

¿Qué lleva el sospechoso? Unscramble the tiles to reveal what the suspect is wearing.

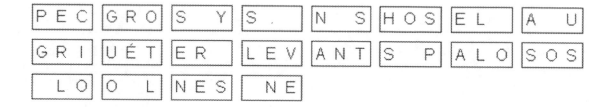

.

¡Así lo pronunciamos!

LL, Y

Both LL and Y have the same pronunciation value as the English *y* in *yes*. In certain dialects, it can be pronounced as the *j* sound in the English word *jump*.

ll	LLAMA	LLENO	CALLE	LLUVIA	ELLOS

y	YO	AYER	YEMA	YESO	YUCATÁN

4. Las partes del coche

The vocabulary in this section will help you to identify some car parts. You will also be able to get a description of a car.

CAR PARTS

el asiento	*seat*	**el tapón**	*hubcap*
el cinturón de seguridad	*seat belt*	**el velocimetro**	*speedometer*
el volante	*steering wheel*	**el cuentakilómetros**	*odometer*
el guardabarros	*fender*	**la guantera**[1]	*glove compartment*
la llanta[2]	*tire*	**el motor**	*motor*
el faro	*headlight*	**el incendido**	*ignition*
el capó	*hood*	**los frenos**	*breaks*
el limpiparabrisas	*winshield wiper*	**los intermitentes**	*turn signals*
el parabrisas	*windshield*	**el espejo retovisor**	*rearview mirror*
la luz de atrás	*tail light*	**el espejo**	*mirror*
el paragolpes	*bumper*		

> [1] also **la cajuelita, la secreta**
>
> [2] also **la goma, el neumático**

VEHICLE INFORMATION

el año	*year*	**la marca**	*make*
el / la chofer	*driver*	**el modelo**	*model*
la clase	*kind*	**la placa**	*license plate*
el tipo	*type*		
de dos puertas	*two-door*	**de cuatro puertas**	*four-door*
el camión	*truck*	**la camioneta**	*van*
la moto(cicleta)	*motorcycle*		

¡Así lo decimos!

Nota gramatical

NUMBERS 101 AND HIGHER

101	ciento uno	1.812	mil ochocientos doce
134	ciento treinta y cuatro	1.982	mil novecientos ochenta y dos
200	doscientos	2.000	dos mil
252	doscientos cincuenta y dos	5.000	cinco mil
300	trescientos	9.000	nueve mil
400	cuatrocientos	1.000.000	un millón
500	quinientos	2.000.000	dos millones
568	quinientos sesenta y ocho		

LOS NÚMEROS ORDINALES	
first	primero
second	segundo
third	tercero
fourth	cuarto
fifth	quinto
sixth	sexto
seventh	séptimo
eighth	octavo
ninth	noveno
tenth	décimo

600	seiscientos
700	setecientos
781	setecientos ochenta y uno
800	ochocientos
900	novecientos
992	novecientos noventa y dos
1.000	mil
1.011	mil once
1.490	mil cuatrocientos noventa
1.783	mil setecientos ochenta y tres

> When the numbers 200 through 900 modify a noun, they must agree in gender: **quinientas mujeres**, **doscientas dos casas**.

✖ Spanish uses periods to indicate thousands and millions, rather than a comma as used in English. A comma is used in place of a decimal point. What we write in English as 1.75 is written in Spanish as **1,75**.

✖ Note that the word **mil** is never pluralized.

✖ **Mil** is never preceded by **un**, but **un** is used with **millón**.

✖ The ordinal numbers are less frequently used in Spanish than in English. The ordinal numbers beyond **décimo** are seldom used.

✖ Ordinal numbers function like adjectives and they have a corresponding feminine form.

    La **segunda** puerta está cerrada.   *The second door is closed.*

✖ Note that the words **primero** and **tercero** shorten when they precede a masculine noun.

    Al **primer** semáforo, doble   *At the first light, turn right.*
               a la derecha .

    Juan vive en el **tercer** piso.   *Juan lives on the third floor.*

Práctica

A. **La palabra secreta**. Unscramble each of the clue words. Copy the letters in the numbered cells to other cells with the same number.

MAGO
    ⬜⬜⬜⬜
        14 11

MALITCOCTEO
    ⬜⬜⬜⬜⬜⬜⬜⬜⬜⬜⬜
              7

LGSEPPAROA
    ⬜⬜⬜⬜⬜⬜⬜⬜⬜⬜
           13

CEFROH
    ⬜⬜⬜⬜⬜⬜
    9

TENLAVO
    ⬜⬜⬜⬜⬜⬜⬜
       19 2

MLEODO
    ⬜⬜⬜⬜⬜⬜
     12 4

TINTISNEEREMT
    ⬜⬜⬜⬜⬜⬜⬜⬜⬜⬜⬜⬜⬜
    10 8   20 5   16

SOETINA
    ⬜⬜⬜⬜⬜⬜⬜
    3   17

LACPA

JICLEAUTA

B. **¿Cómo es el vehículo?** Bring in a picture of a car. Answer the questions below.

1. ¿Qué clase de vehículo es?

   _____.

2. ¿Cuál es la marca y el modelo?

   _____.

3. ¿Cuántas puertas tiene?

   _____.

4. ¿De qué color es?

   _____.

5. ¿De qué año es?

   _____.

6. ¿Cuál es el número de la placa?

   _____.

C. **Las placas**. Your instructor will read 4 license plates. Write down the letters and numbers that you hear. Each license plate will be said twice.

D. **¿Qué número es?** Read the following numbers aloud in Spanish.

1. 102
2. 935
3. 4.000.000
4. 1.784
5. 550.875
6. 18.356
7. 555
8. 12.333.586
9. 2.097

Just for fun

¿Cuánto cuesta? How much would the following items cost? Compare your prices with those of your classmates.

1. un estéreo Aiwa
2. una computadora Dell
3. un reloj Timex
4. unos zapatos de tennis Nike
5. un iPod Touch

¡Así lo pronunciamos!

M, N, Ñ

| **m** | M has the same pronunciation as the English *m* in *mother*. |

| MANEJAR | METRO | AMERICANO | MOTOR | MUSLO |

| **n** | N has the same pronunciation as the English *n*. |

| NAVAJA | NEGRO | NIÑO | NOMBRE | NUNCA |

| **ñ** | Ñ has a pronunciation similar to the English *ny* in *canyon*. |

| CAÑÓN | MONTAÑA | AÑO | NIÑERA | CAÑA |

Description

Vocabulario útil

✖ **¿Fue un niño, adolescente o adulto?**
Was it a child, teen or adult?

✖ **¿Fue hombre o mujer?**
Was it a man or a woman?

✖ **¿Estaba cubierta la cara?**
Was his/her face covered?

✖ **¿Puede decirme . . .**   *Can you tell me (the) . . .*
  la edad?   *age?*
  el color de los ojos?   *eye color?*
  el color del pelo?   *hair color?*
  la estatura?   *height?*
  la raza?   *race?*
  el tamaño?   *size?*
  el color del piel?   *skin color?*
  el peso?   *weight?*

Vehicle Stop

✖ **Necesito ver su licencia de manejar**[1] **y el registro de carro**[2].
I need to see your driver's license and car registration.

✖ **¿Ud. Sabe por qué lo paré?**
Do you know why I stopped you?

> ✖ **Pasó por la luz roja**.
> *You went through the red light.*

> ✖ **No tenía el derecho de vía**.
> *You didn't have the right of way.*

> ✖ **No obedeció la señal**.
> *You didn't obey the sign.*

> ✖ **Estaba manejando**[3] **muy rápido**.
> *You were driving too fast.*

[1] also **permiso de conducir**
[2] also **coche**
[3] also **conduciendo**

CONTINUED . . .

✖ **Estaba virando bruscamente**.
You were swerving.

✖ **Ud. tiene una placa falsa en el carro**.
You have a false license plate on your car.

✖ **La luz de atrás izquierda (derecha) no funciona**.
Your left (right) tail light isn't working.

✖ **Han caducado sus placas**.
Your plates have expired.

✖ **Han caducado sus calcomanías**.
Your decals have expired.

✖ **¿Sabe el límite de velocidad?**
Do you know the speed limit?

✖ **¿Sabe cuán rápido estaba manejando?**
Do you know how fast you were driving?

✖ **Ha caducado su licencia**.
Your license has expired.

✖ **Su licencia ha sido cancelada**.
Your license has been revoked

✖ **No puede manejar[1] sin licencia**.
You cannot drive without a license.

[1] also **conducir**

Regular Verbs

AR				ER	
acusar	to accuse	**matar**	to kill	**aprender**	to learn
alimentar	to feed	**pagar**	to pay for	**beber**	to drink
alquilar	to rent	**pegar**	to hit	**correr**	to run
apuñalar	to stab	**patrullar**	to patrol	**creer**	to believe
asesinar	to murder	**pintar**	to paint	**leer**	to read
asustar	to frighten	**quemar**	to burn	**meter**	to put into
calmar	to calm	**recuperar**	to recover	**prometer**	to promise
cambiar	to change	**regañar**	to scold	**vender**	to sell
caminar	to walk	**registrar**	to search		
comprar	to buy	**remolcar**	to tow	IR	
desmayar	to faint	**rodear**	to surround	**abrir**	to open
empujar	to push	**sacar**	to take out	**admitir**	to admit
escuchar	to listen to	**saludar**	to greet	**asistir (a)**	to attend
esperar	to wait for	**sangrar**	to bleed	**decidir**	to decide
estacionar	to park	**secar**	to dry	**discutir**	to discuss
estudiar	to study	**señalar**	to signal	**escribir**	to write
examinar	to examine	**sudar**	to sweat	**recibir**	to receive
gritar	to yell	**terminar**	to end	**subir**	to climb
hablar	to speak	**testificar**	to testify	**sufrir**	to suffer
inhalar	to inhale	**trabajar**	to work	**vivir**	to live
inyectar	to inject	**usar**	to use		
jalar	to pull	**verificar**	to check		
limpiar	to clean	**viajar**	to travel		
llamar	to call	**violar**	to rape		
llegar	to arrive	**zigzaguear**	to swerve		
mandar	to send				
manejar	to drive				

Un poco de todo 2

1. Spanish in the United States

You don't have to go to Chile or Panama to encounter people who speak Spanish on a daily basis. There are more than 45 million people of Hispanic descent living in the United States. In fact, the U.S. is now the fifth largest Spanish-speaking country in the world. There are 10 states that have almost 87% of the total Hispanic population.

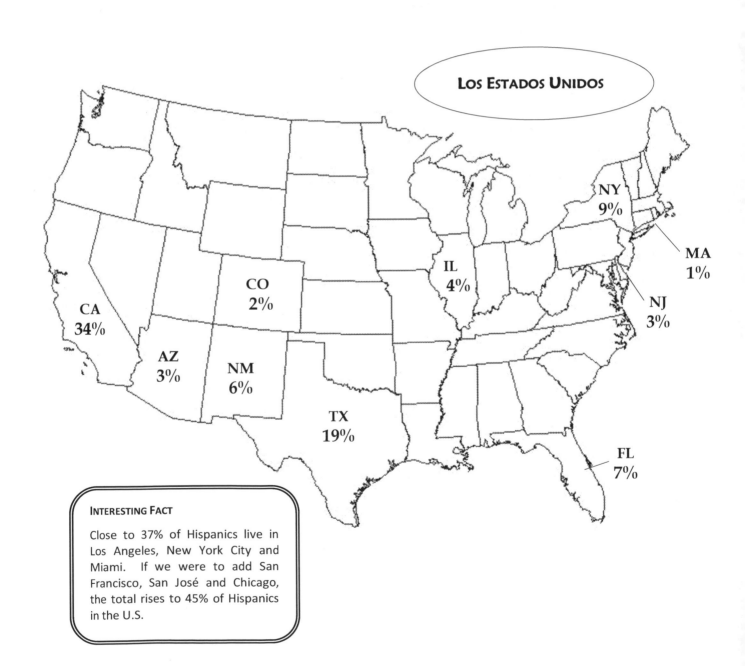

LOS ESTADOS UNIDOS

NY 9%

MA 1%

IL 4%

CO 2%

CA 34%

NJ 3%

AZ 3%

NM 6%

TX 19%

FL 7%

INTERESTING FACT

Close to 37% of Hispanics live in Los Angeles, New York City and Miami. If we were to add San Francisco, San José and Chicago, the total rises to 45% of Hispanics in the U.S.

U.S. CITIES AND STATES WITH SPANISH NAMES

Spanish explorers in the New World gave many of our states and cities Spanish names. Since Spain is a Catholic country, the explorers sometimes named the town or region after the saint whose feast was celebrated on the day they arrived. Other names tell us the explorers' impressions of the physical characteristics of the land or its formation.

- **San Francisco** was named after St. Francis because it was founded on his day.

- **Colorado**, which means *reddish*, was given its name because of the reddish color of the earth.

- **El Paso**, which means *the pass*, was named by Juan de Oñate for its strategic location at a narrow pass on the Río Grande.

- **Florida** was named for Easter Sunday, or *Pascua Florida*, by Ponce de León who arrived there on that day.

Match the cities with the states in which they are found. Note that both the cities and the states have Spanish names.

_____ 1. San Agustín

_____ 2. San Francisco

_____ 3. El Paso

_____ 4. Los Ángeles

_____ 5. Boca Ratón

_____ 6. San Diego

_____ 7. Albuquerque

_____ 8. Pueblo

_____ 9. San Antonio

_____ 10. Amarillo

_____ 11. Las Vegas

_____ 12. Santa Fe

a. TEXAS

b. NUEVO MÉXICO

c. FLORIDA

d. CALIFORNIA

e. NEVADA

f. COLORADO

REGIONAL DIVERSITY

There is great regional diversity among U.S. Hispanics. Many people of Mexican descent inhabit the Southwestern part of the United States, including population as far north as Colorado. Large groups of Puerto Ricans can be found in New York while Florida is a host to a large Cuban and Central American population. More recent immigrants include Nicaraguan and Salvadorans, who have established large communities in many U.S. cities, among them San Francisco and Los Angeles.

2. Las palabras interrogativas

Question words are very important for law enforcement officials. They help to gather much-needed information in any situation. Use them as often as possible.

¿Cómo?	*How?*	**¿Qué?**	*What?*
¿Cuál?	*Which?*	**¿Quién?**	*Who?*
¿Cuándo?	*When?*	**¿A qué hora?**	*At what time?*
¿Cuánto?	*How much, many?*	**¿Para qué?**	*Why?*
¿Dónde?	*Where?*	**¿Por qué?**	*Why?*

✖ **¿Qué?** is used when asking for a *definition*, *description* or *explanation*. It is also used before a noun when you want to ask *which?*.	¿Qué es esto? *What is this?* ¿Qué haces? *What are you doing?* ¿Qué libro quieres? *Which book do you want?*
✖ **¿Cuál?** also means *which*. It has two forms and is used when asking for a *choice* or a *selection*.	¿Cuál es su dirección? *What's your address?* ¿Cuáles son los meses del año? *What are the months of the year?*
✖ **¿Por qué?** is used when asking *because of what?*.	¿Por qué no viene con nosotros? *Why doesn't he come with us?* - Porque no quiere. *Because he doesn't want to.*
✖ **¿Para qué?** is used when asking *for what purpose?*.	¿Para qué necesitas una pistola? *Why do you need a pistol?* - Para protegerme. *To protect myself.* **CONTINUED . . .**

✖ **¿Cuándo?** asks for a general time.	¿Cuándo viene Juan? *When is Juan coming?* - Mañana por la mañana. *Tomorrow morning.*
✖ **¿A qué hora?** asks for a specific time.	¿A qué hora viene Juan? *At what time is Juan coming?* - Viene a las seis en punto. *He's coming at 6:00 sharp.*
✖ Prepositions can also be added to some question words to obtain more information.	**¿A quién** llamas? *Whom are you calling?* **¿Con quién** trabajas? *With whom do you work?* **¿De quién** es el carro? *Whose car is this?* **¿Adónde** va Miguel? *Where is Miguel going?* **¿De dónde** es Jaime? *Where is Jaime from?*

A. **Preguntas.** Fill in each blank with the correct Spanish interrogative pronoun.

1. ¿ _____ es Miguel? – **Es rubio, alto y delgado**.

2. ¿ _____ mujeres hay aquí? – **Treinta y seis**.

3. ¿ _____ es la clase de español? – **Los martes y jueves**.

4. ¿ _____ es su número de teléfono? – **6873379**.

5. ¿ _____ nació Juan (*was Juan born*)? – **En Puerto Rico**.

6. ¿ _____ estudia español? – **Porque es necesario**.

7. ¿ _____ vienen los sospechosos? – **A las tres de la tarde**.

8. ¿ _____ es el camión? – **Es de mi amigo**.

9. ¿ _____ es él? – **Es mi vecino** (*neighbor*).

3. Los verbos regulares (-ar, -er, -ir)

B. **Rompecabezas**. Write the present tense of each verb in the puzzle below.

ACROSS
1. yo (correr)
7. nosotros (creer)
8. ella (leer)
10. Ud. (preguntar)
13. nosotros (abrir)
14. yo (recuperar)
15. yo (asistir)
17. ella (necesitar)
21. tú (contestar)
22. ellos (vender)

DOWN
2. ella (recibir)
3. ella (tomar)
4. ellos (discutir)
5. ellas (meter)
6. nosotros (gritar)
9. yo (sufrir)
11. nosotros (trabajar)
12. él (aprender)
16. nosotros (beber)
18. ellos (escribir)
19. Ud. (beber)
20. nosotros (caminar)

4. Las partes del cuerpo

C. **¿Qué parte del cuerpo es?** Name each part of the body in the outline below.

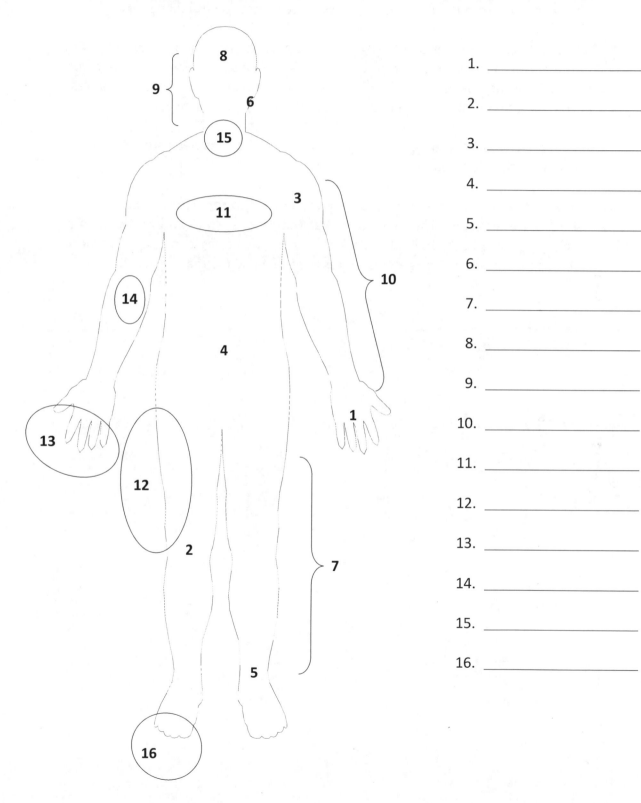

1. _____

2. _____

3. _____

4. _____

5. _____

6. _____

7. _____

8. _____

9. _____

10. _____

11. _____

12. _____

13. _____

14. _____

15. _____

16. _____

5. Situaciones

D. **¡Ayúdeme, por favor!** Working with a partner, act out each situation below. Be sure to use vocabulary from the first two chapters, as well as a Spanish dictionary.

1. A young Hispanic man is on the ground holding his stomach and needs help. Tell him that you don't speak Spanish very well. Ask if he speaks English. When you find out that he doesn't, ask him to speak Spanish slowly. Get his name, address and telephone number. Tell him that the ambulance is on the way.

2. A woman has come to the station to report that her car has been stolen. Ask the make, model, color, year and license number.

3. Central Bank has just been robbed. Someone calls to report the robbery. You ask for a description. The caller says that the man is white and the woman is black. They are both dressed in dark clothes and wearing caps. Ask for more detailed information. You get the address of the bank and thank the caller.

Introduction

This chapter will give you the skills and practice necessary to gain control of a situation. Domestic violence, family members, and breaking and entering vocabulary will also be presented in this chapter.

In This Chapter

COMUNICACIÓN

- ☑ **Arrest expressions**
- ☑ **Weapons**
- ☑ **Domestic violence**
- ☑ **Giving directions**
- ☑ **Places in the city**
- ☑ **Family**
- ☑ **Parts of the house**
- ☑ **Appliances**
- ☑ **Jewelry**
- ☑ **Breaking and entering**
- ☑ **Verbs of obligation**

ESTRUCTURAS

- ☑ **Stem-changing verbs**
- ☑ **The personal A**
- ☑ **Direct object pronouns**
- ☑ **ESTAR**
- ☑ **IR**
- ☑ **Verbs irregular in the YO form**
- ☑ **Possessive adjectives**

PRONUNCIACIÓN

- ☑ **K, Q**
- ☑ **G, J**
- ☑ **L, R, RR**
- ☑ **F, W**

LA ADVERTENCIA MIRANDA

Antes de hacerle alguna pregunta, Ud. debe entender cuales son sus derechos.

1. Ud. tiene el derecho de guardar (mantener) silencio.

2. Cualquier cosa que diga, puede usarse y se usará en contra de Ud. en una corte.

3. Ud. tiene el derecho de hablar con un abogado y tenerlo presente cuando se le interroga.

4. Si Ud. no puede pagar un abogado, se le nombrará uno para presentarle durante cualquier interrogación, sí así lo desea Ud.

5. Ud. puede decidir en cualquier momento ejercer estos derechos y no contestar ninguna pregunta ni hacer ninguna declaración.

¿Comprende cada uno de los derechos que yo le he explicado? Teniendo en cuenta estos derechos, ¿quiere Ud. hablar con nosotros ahora?

1. ¡Manos arriba!

In this section you will learn those command expressions that help you gain control of a situation. These expressions are important when an emergency arises.

COMMAND EXPRESSIONS

¡Así lo decimos!

¡Policía! ¡No se mueva!	*Police! Don't move!*
¡Párese o disparo!	*Stop or I'll shoot!*
¡Mantenga las manos . . .	*Keep your hands . . .*
en el suelo!	*on the ground!*
donde las puedo ver!	*where I can see them!*
encima de la cabeza!	*on top of your head!*
detrás del cuello!	*behind your neck!*
con las palmas arriba!	*with the palms up!*
¡Muévase muy despacio!	*Move very slowly!*
¡Separe las piernas!	*Spread your legs!*
¡Cruce los pies!	*Cross your feet!*
¡Cállese!	*Be quiet!*
¡Salga con las manos arriba!	*Get out with your hands up!*
¡Ponga el arma en el suelo!	*Put your weapon on the ground!*
¡Arrodíllese y quédese allí!	*Kneel down and stay there!*
¡Acuéstese en el estómago!	*Lie on your stomach!*
¡Voltéese y camine hacia atrás!	*Turn around and walk backwards!*
¡Cálmese!	*Calm down!*
¡Quieto(a)!	*Freeze!*
¡Usted está arrestado(a)!	*You are under arrest!*

WEAPONS

¡Suelte . . .	*Drop . . .*
el palo de béisbol!	*the baseball bat!*
la navaja!	*the blade!*

¡Suelte . . .	Drop . . .
la botella!	*the bottle*!
el ladrillo!	*the brick*!
la daga!	*the dagger*!
el arma de fuego!	*the firearm*!
el martillo!	*the hammer*!
el hacha!	*the hachet*!
el cuchillo!	*the knife*!
la ametralladora!	*the machine gun*!
el tubo!	*the pipe*!
la pistola!	*the pistol*!
el revólver!	*the revolver*!
el rifle!	*the rifle*!
el serrucho!	*the saw*!
las tijeras!	*scissors*!
el atornillador!	*screwdriver*!
la escopeta!	*shot gun*!
la espada!	*sword*!
la llave inglesa!	*wrench*!
la bomba!	*the bomb*!

Nota gramatical

STEM-CHANGING VERBS

There are some verbs that are regular, but the vowel changes when the verb is conjugated. These verbs are known as **stem-changing verbs**. They undergo a change in the stressed vowel of the stem when it is conjugated. The ending for stem-changing verbs are the same as those of regular –**ar**, –**er** and –**ir** verbs. The only difference is that the stem vowels are stressed in all present tense forms except **nosotros**. Look at the verbs on the next page.

CERRAR (TO CLOSE)		[e > ie]
yo **cie**rro	nosotros cerramos	
tú **cie**rras		
él ella **cie**rra Ud.	ellos ellas **cie**rran Uds.	

VOLVER (TO RETURN)		[o > ue]
yo **vue**lvo	nosotros volvemos	
tú **vue**lves		
él ella **vue**lve Ud.	ellos ellas **vue**lven Uds.	

PEDIR (TO ASK FOR)		[e > i]
yo **pi**do	nosotros pedimos	
tú **pi**des		
él ella **pi**de Ud.	ellos ellas **pi**den Uds.	

VOLVER (TO RETURN)		[u > ue]
yo **jue**go	nosotros jugamos	
tú **jue**gas		
él ella **jue**ga Ud.	ellos ellas **jue**gan Uds.	

✖ **Jugar** is the only **u** > **ue** stem-changing verb in the Spanish language.

✖ The verbs **empezar** and **comenzar** are followed by the preposition **a** to express that something is about to start.

Él empieza a decir la verdad. *He's beginning to tell the truth.*

✖ **Volver** when followed by the preposition **a** means to do something again.

La mujer vuelve a llorar. *The woman is crying again.*

✖ **Pensar** when followed by an infinitive means *to plan on doing something.* When followed by the preposition **en**, it means *to think about (doing) something.*

Piensan llamar a la policía. *They plan on calling the police.*

Pienso en mi vida. *I am thinking about my life.*

¿Piensas en salir? *You're thinking about leaving?*

✖ **Perder** can mean *to lose* or *to miss (train, bus).*

Ella va a perder las llaves. *She's going to loose the keys.*

No quiero perder el tren. *I don't want to miss the train.*

✖ **Seguir** and its derivatives are irregular in the **yo** form: **sigo**, sigues, sigue, seguimos, siguen.

Práctica

A. **Situaciones.** What would you say in the following situations?

1. A man that you have just pulled over gets out of his car and reaches into his coat pocket.
2. You want a suspect to stop. Tell him halt or you'll shoot. Another man appears. Tell him to freeze.
3. You see a teenager who is vandalizing cars. Identify yourself as a police officer and tell him to halt. Inform him that he is under arrest.

B. **Los verbos**. Conjugate each verb below in the present tense.

	CONTAR	MENTIR	SERVIR
yo	_____	_____	_____
tú	_____	_____	_____
él ⎫ ella ⎬ Ud. ⎭	_____	_____	_____
nosotros	_____	_____	_____
ellos ⎫ ellas ⎬ Uds. ⎭	_____	_____	_____

MÁS PRÁCTICA

Complete verb charts **C – F** in the appendix.

C. **Más verbos**. Rewrite each sentence with the correct present tense form of the verb in bold print.

1. Las guardias **PERSEGUIR** al criminal.

   _____.

2. Yo **CERRAR** las maletas.

   _____.

3. Él **PODER** terminar el trabajo en seguida.

   _____.

4. ¿Qué **PENSAR** Ud.?

   _____.

5. La policía **REPETIR** la pregunta.

   _____.

6. Uds. no **RECORDAR** el episodio.

_____.

7. Yo **PEDIR** una ración de papas fritas.

_____.

8. El viejo **MORIR** en el hospital.

_____.

9. Miguel no **ENTENDER** la situación.

_____.

10. Mi hijo nunca **MENTIR**.

_____.

Just for fun

Un arma peligrosa. Unscramble each of the weapon words below. Copy the letters in the numbered cells to other cells with the same number.

MORTADALARLAE

		3		7									

IRTAJSE

			9		4	

LICLOUHC

5	1		6				

TIPSOAL

			8			

NRLADTAROILO

			2								

1	2

3	4	5	6	7	8	9

¡Así lo pronunciamos!

K, Q

K is only found in words borrowed from other languages and has the same pronunciation as the English letter *k*.

KILO   KANSAS

q

Q is only used in the combination with **ue** and **ui**, with u being silent. It has the same pronunciation as the English *k* in *kick*.

QUEBRAR   QUEJA   QUEMADURA   QUINCE   ATAQUE

2. La violencia doméstica

This section will help you to ask questions about domestic violence. These questions and phrases will help you to get things started.

¡Así lo decimos!

¿Cuál de ustedes llamó?	*Which one of you called?*
¿Hay alguien herido?	*Is anyone hurt?*
¿Necesita ayuda?	*Do you need help?*
¿Qué pasó?	*What happened?*
¿Qué le hizo?	*What did he do to you?*
Me pegó.	*He hit me.*
Me apuñaló.	*He stabbed me.*
Me empujó.	*He pushed me.*
Me cortó.	*He cut me.*
Me mordió.	*He bit me.*
Me dio una patada.	*He kicked me.*
Me dio una bofetada.	*He slapped me.*
Me dio un puñetazo.	*He punched me.*
¿Es él una persona violenta?	*Is he a violent person?*
¿Cómo está relacionada con él?	*What's your relationship to him?*
Soy su . . .	*I'm his . . .*
esposa.	*wife.*
novia.	*girlfriend.*
pareja.	*partner.*
amiga.	*friend.*
¿Están . . .	*Are you . . .*
viviendo juntos?	*living together?*
casados?	*married?*
divorciados?	*divorced?*
separados?	*separated?*

¿Está borracho o drogado?	*Is he drunk or on drugs?*
¿Hay armas de fuego adentro?	*Are there any firearms inside?*
¿Ha pasado esto antes?	*Has this happened before?*
¿Ha llamado antes?	*Have you called before?*
¿Cuántas veces?	*How many times?*
¿Quiere . . .	*Do you want . . .*
una orden de arresto?	*an arrest warrant?*
una orden del tribunal?	*a court order?*
presentar la acusación?	*press charges?*
hacerle cargos?	*press charges?*
que le arreste?	*me to arrest him?*
¡No grite!	*Don't yell!*
¡Venga acá!	*Come here!*
¡Baje eso!	*Put that down!*
¡Vamos al otro cuarto!	*Let's go to the other room.*
¿Estará bien si me voy?	*Would it be OK if I leave?*
¿Tiene un lugar adónde ir?	*Do you have a place to go?*
¿Qué quiere que haga?	*What do you want me to do?*
No puede pegarle a su esposa.	*You can't hit your wife.*
Es contra la ley.	*It's against the law.*

Nota gramatical

THE PERSONAL A

The personal **a** is used in Spanish before a direct object that is a specific person. The word **a** has no equivalent in English. Compare the two sentences below.

Mario escucha la radio.	*Mario is listening to the radio.*
Mario admira **a** su hermano.	*Mario admires his brother.*

✖ Use the personal **a** when the direct object is a pet. **A + el** contracts to **al**.

El niño busca **al** gato.   *The child is looking for the cat.*

✖ After the verb TENER, the personal **a** is generally not used.

Tenemos muchos amigos.   *We have a lot of friends.*

✖ The personal **a** is used before the interrogative words **¿quién?** and **¿quiénes?** when they function as direct objects.

¿A quién llamas?   *Whom are you calling?*

DIRECT OBJECT PRONOUNS

A direct object (**un complemento directo**) is the direct receiver of the action of the verb. It answers the question **who?** or **what?**. The direct object pronouns used in Spanish are listed in the chart below.

SINGULAR	PLURAL
me *me*	**nos** *us*
te *you*	
lo *you, him, it*	**los** *you, them*
la *you, her, it*	**las** *you, them*

✖ Direct object pronouns agree in number and gender with the nouns they replace.

La policía busca a **los niños**.   *The police are looking for the children.*
La policía **los** busca.   *The police are looking for them.*

✖ Direct object pronouns are usually placed before the conjugated verb

¿Quiere Ud. **una orden de arresto**?   *Do you want an arrest warrant?*
Sí, **la** quiero.   *Yes, I want it.*

✖ In negative sentences, the pronoun is placed between **no** and the conjugated verb.

¿Busca **al gato** el niño?

Is the child looking for the cat?

No, no **lo** busca.

No, he isn't looking for it.

✖ Third person direct object pronouns are only used when the direct object noun has already been mentioned.

Necesito **un cuchillo** y
  lo necesito ahora.

I need a knife and I need it now.

✖ When the verb is in the infinitive construction, the pronoun can be placed before the conjugated verb or attached to the infinitive.

Miguel quiere vender **drogas**.

Miguel wants to sell drugs.

Miguel **las** quiere vender.
Miguel quiere vender**las**.

Miguel wants to sell them.

Práctica

A. **Situaciones.** What would you say in the following situations?

1. You answer a 911 call about a case of domestic violence. When you arrive, there is a man and a woman on the patio screaming. They are both drunk and wounded.
2. A neighbor called because she heard a woman scream. When you get to the house, the husband opens the door and you cannot see his wife. He says that nothing is going on and that you can't enter.
3. You arrive at a residence where there was a fight. The father and the 10-year old son were fighting. The mother made the phone call. The father and son both have bleeding faces and it appears that the son's nose is broken.

B. **La a personal.** Complete each statement by filling in the blanks with the personal **a** if needed. Watch for the contraction **al**.

1. Tomás espera _____ amigo de Nina.

2. Los niños comen _____ el almuerzo en la escuela.

3. Julieta y Maricarmen invitan _____ Alfonso a comer.

4. A las 3:00 los estudiantes visitan _____ profesor Sánchez, que está enfermo.

5. No me gusta cuidar _____ mi hermano.

6. Muchas veces escuchas _____ la radio por la noche.

7. Uds. buscan _____ el carro mañana.

8. Los martes, siempre llamo _____ mi abuela por teléfono.

C. **Los complementos directos**. Rewrite each sentence below, replacing the direct object noun in bold print with a direct object pronoun.

1. El coche tiene **una placa falsa**.

   _____.

2. Los niños usan **los cinturones de seguridad**.

   _____.

3. Ud. necesita obedecer **las reglas**.

   _____.

   _____.

4. Los bomberos controlan **el fuego**.

   _____.

5. Yo miro **la television**.

   _____.

6. Mi amigo vende **casas**.

   _____.

7. Las policías dirigen **el tráfico**.

_____ .

8. Los jóvenes no pueden comprar **cigarillos**.

_____ .

_____ .

9. Muchas personas quieren tener **armas de fuego** en su casa.

_____ .

_____ .

Just for fun

La violencia doméstica. You answer a 911 call about a case of domestic violence. When you get there, Sandra Escóbar's husband has already left. Unscramble the tiles to reveal what type of person her husband is and what he did to her.

UNA	M	TA .	EL	ES	VIO	NA	PE

BO	ADA	FET	E D	LEN	RSO	.	UNA

I O

_____ .

_____ .

¡Así lo pronunciamos!

G, J

g	G has two sounds in Spanish. When it is before **a**, **o**, **u**, **l** or **r** it has a *g* sound, as in the English word *go*.

| GATO | GOMA | GUITARRA | GLOBO | GRIFO |

Before the letters **i** and **e**, G has the *h* sound as in the English word *hot*.

| GIMNASIO | GENTE | GIRAFA | GEL | GEMELO |

j	J has the same pronunciation as the English *h* in *hot*.

| CAJA | JUEVES | JAMÓN | RELOJ | JERINGA |

3. Dando direcciones

Giving directions is another part of your job as a police officer. Learn how to give directions in Spanish.

ASKING DIRECTIONS

¿Me podría decir cómo llegar a . . .?	*Can you tell me how to get to . . .?*
¿Dónde está . . .?	*Where is . . .?*
¿Dónde queda . . .?	

GIVING DIRECTIONS

Está . . . cuadras de aquí.	*It's . . . blocks from here.*
Tome la calle . . .	*Take . . . Street.*
Siga la calle . . . hasta . . .	*Follow . . . Street to . . .*
Doble a la derecha (izquierda) en la calle . . .	*Turn right (left) at . . . Street.*
Siga derecho.	*Go straight.*
Cruce la avenida . . .	*Cross . . . Avenue.*
Camine dos cuadras hasta . . .	*Walk two blocks to . . .*
El edifico está a mano derecha (izquierda).	*The building is on the right-(left-) hand side.*

PREPOSITIONS

al lado de	*next to; beside*	**delante de**	*in front of*
a la derecha de	*to the right of*	**detrás de**	*behind*
a la izquierda de	*to the left of*	**encima de**	*on top of*
en	*in; on*	**enfrente de**	*in front of*
cerca de	*near*	**entre**	*between; among*
con	*with*	**lejos de**	*far from*
debajo de	*below*	**sobre**	*on; over*

¡Así lo decimos!

PLACES IN THE CITY

la estación de bomberos, el parque de bomberos	*fire station*
el banco	*bank*
la iglesia	*church*
el hospital	*hospital*
el parque	*park*
el palacio municipal, la alcadía, el ayuntamiento	*city hall*
el tribunal, la corte	*courthouse*
la estación de policía, la comisaría	*police station*
la oficina de correos	*post office*
la escuela	*school*
el cementerio	*cemetery*

Nota gramatical

ESTAR

In lesson 2, you learned how to conjugate and use the verb SER (*to be*). You will now learn a second verb that means *to be*, the verb ESTAR. This verb is irregular and its forms must be memorized. ESTAR has many uses in the Spanish language.

ESTAR (TO BE)			
yo	**estoy**	nosotros	**estamos**
tú	**estás**		
él ella Ud.	**estás**	ellos ellas Uds.	**están**

✖ **Condition** (usually the product of a change)

La casa está sucia.   *The house is dirty.*

✖ **Location**

Las montañas están lejos.   *The mountains are far away.*

✖ **Estar** is used with adjectives to describe the physical conditions of places and things. It is also used with adjectives to describe how people feel. Listed below are adjectives that describe emotions and conditions.

abierto/a	*opened*	**equivocado/a**	*wrong*
aburrido/a	*bored*	**feliz**	*happy*
alegre	*happy*	**limpio/a**	*clean*
avergonzado/a	*embarrassed*	**listo/a**	*ready*
cansado/a	*tired*	**nervioso/a**	*nervous*
cerrado/a	*closed*	**ocupado/a**	*busy*
cómodo/a	*comfortable*	**ordenado/a**	*orderly*
contento/a	*happy, content*	**preocupado/a (por)**	*worried (about)*
desordenado/a	*disorderly*	**seguro/a**	*sure*
enamorado/a (de)	*in love (with)*	**sucio/a**	*dirty*
enojado/a	*mad, angry*	**triste**	*sad*

IR

The verb IR means *to go*. This verb is irregular and its forms must be memorized.

IR (TO GO)			
yo	**voy**	nosotros	**vamos**
tú	**vas**		
él ella Ud.	**va**	ellos ellas Uds.	**van**

✖ **Ir** is used with the preposition **a** to express destination.

Vamos **a** la gasolinera.   *We're going to the gas station.*

Tú vas **al** banco.   *You are going to the bank.*

✖ This verb is also used to talk about actions that are going to happen in the near future. [**ir + a + infinitive**]

Juan **va a llamar** a la policía.   *Juan's going to call the police.*

VERBS IRREGULAR IN THE YO FORM

Several commonly used verbs have irregular **yo** forms in the present tense.

HACER (TO DO, MAKE)		
yo **hago**	nosotros	hacemos
tú haces		
él	ellos	
ella hace	ellas	hacen
Ud.	Uds.	

OÍR (TO HEAR)		
yo **oigo**	nosotros	oímos
tú oyes		
él	ellos	
ella oye	ellas	oyen
Ud.	Uds.	

PONER (TO PUT, PLACE)		
yo **pongo**	nosotros	ponemos
tú pones		
él	ellos	
ella pone	ellas	ponen
Ud.	Uds.	

Poner can also mean *to turn on appliances.*

Mi hermana no quiere poner la televisión. *My sister doesn't want to turn on the TV.*

SALIR (TO LEAVE)	
yo **salgo**	nosotros salimos
tú sales	
él	ellos
ella sale	ellas salen
Ud.	Uds.

Salir changes meaning with a preposition.

Ella sale **del** cuarto. *She's leaving the room.*

Juan sale **con** Marta. *Juan's going out with Marta.*

Mi familia sale **para** México hoy. *My family is leaving for Mexico today.*

TRAER (TO BRING)	
yo **traigo**	nosotros traemos
tú traes	
él	ellos
ella trae	ellas traen
Ud.	Uds.

DECIR (TO SAY, TELL)	
yo **digo**	nosotros decimos
tú dices	
él	ellos
ella dice	ellas dicen
Ud.	Uds.

VENIR (TO COME)	
yo **vengo**	nosotros venimos
tú vienes	
él	ellos
ella viene	ellas vienen
Ud.	Uds.

Práctica

A. **¿Ser o estar?** Rewrite each sentence with the correct form of **ser** or **estar**. Review the forms and uses of **ser** on pages 43 – 44.

1. Nosotros . . . norteamericanos.

   _____.

2. Las montañas . . . muy lejos.

   _____.

3. ¿ . . . Ud. listo para salir?

   _____.

4. Hoy . . . sábado.

   _____.

5. Estos productos . . . de Cuba.

   _____.

6. El museo . . . enfrente del parque.

   _____.

7. Las ventanas . . . limpias.

   _____.

8. La corbata de Ernesto . . . de colores muy vivos.

   _____.

B. **Más lugares.** Tell where each of the following people is going. Use the correct form of the verb **ir**. Follow the model.

MODELO   Yo / lavandería   *Yo voy a la lavandería.*

1. tú / hospital

   _____.

2. Miguel / gasolinera

   _____.

3. nosotros / la estación de policía

   _____.

4. yo / gimnasio

   _____.

5. ellos / teatro

   _____.

C. **¿Qué van a hacer?** Tell what each of the people below is going to do. Follow the model.

   MODELO   Juan escribe una carta.   *Juan va a escribir una carta.*

1. La policía arresta al criminal.

   _____.

2. Nosotros alquilamos un coche.

   _____.

3. Yo firmo la multa

   _____.

4. Los niños usan los cinturones de seguridad.

   _____.

5. Tú vas esta semana a la corte.

_____.

D. **¡Así es la gente!** People are different in many ways. Rewrite the following sentences with the present tense of the verb in bold print. This exercise is on the next page.

1. Marcos **VER** a Elena los sábados, pero yo **VER** a María los domingos.

_____

_____.

2. Tú **PONER** el radio cuando estudias, pero yo **PONER** la televisión cuando estudio.

_____

_____.

3. Nosotros **HACER** la tarea por la mañana, pero tú **HACER** la tarea por la noche.

_____

_____.

4. Yo **SALIR** esta noche, pero Juan **SALIR** mañana.

_____

_____.

5. Fernán **OÍR** muy bien, pero la Señora Vargas no **OÍR** muy bien.

_____

_____.

6. Ernesto **TRAER** un diccionario a clase, pero yo **TRAER** papel.

_____

_____.

7. Los jóvenes DECIR mentiras, pero yo siempre DECIR la verdad.

_____

_____.

Just for fun

Necesito direcciones. A Latino asks you how to get somewhere and the distance of this place from where he is now. Unscramble the tiles below to find out the two questions that he is asking you.

N D E	Q U	U Í ?	¿ D Ó	M U N	J O S	I C I	A Q
DE	T Á	¿ E S	E L	M U Y	P A	L ?	E D A
I O	P A	L E	L A C

_____?

_____?

¡Así lo pronunciamos!

L, R, RR

| l |

L has almost the same pronunciation as the English *l* in *love*.

| LADRÓN | LAGO | LÍDER | LITRO | LUGAR |

| r |

R has the same pronunciation as the English *dd* in *ladder*.

| CARA | PERO | ARENA | HERIR | ARETE |

At the beginning of a word and after **l**, **n**, or **s**, R it is pronounced with a strong trill.

| RADAR | ALREDEDOR | ENRIQUE | ISRAEL | RUBIO |

| rr |

RR is pronounced with a strong trill.

| CARRO | PERRO | BURRO | ARRIBA | SIERRA |

4. La familia y las partes de la casa

When responding to a domestic call, it's necessary to establish the relationship of the people involved in the dispute. This section will present vocabulary for family members and the parts of the house.

¡Así lo decimos!

FAMILY MEMBERS

el abuelo	*grandfather*	**la abuela**	*grandmother*
el padre	*father*	**la madre**	*mother*
el hijo	*son*	**la hija**	*daughter*
el hermano	*brother*	**la hermana**	*sister*
el tío	*uncle*	**la tía**	*aunt*
el primo	*cousin (male)*	**la prima**	*cousin (female)*
el novio	*boyfriend*	**la novia**	*girlfriend*
el esposo, marido	*husband*	**la esposa, mujer**	*wife*
el cuñado	*brother-in-law*	**la cuñada**	*sister-in-law*
el nieto	*grandson*	**la nieta**	*granddaughter*
el suegro	*father-in-law*	**la suegra**	*mother-in-law*
el sobrino	*nephew*	**la sobrina**	*niece*
el yerno	*son-in-law*	**la nuera**	*daugher-in-law*

PLURALS

los abuelos	*grandparents*	**los padres**	*parents*
los hijos	*children*	**los hermanos**	*brothers*
los tíos	*aunt and uncle*	**los primos**	*cousins*
los novios	*sweethearts*	**los esposos**	*husband and wife*
		las esposas	*wives, handcuffs*

PARTS OF THE HOUSE

el salón	*living room*	**la cocina**	*kitchen*
el cuarto	*bedroom*	**el garaje**	*garage*
el ático, altillo	*attic*	**el sótano**	*basement*
el baño	*bathroom*	**la puerta**	*door*
la ventana	*window*		

HOME ENTERTAINMENT

el televisor	*television*	**el radio**	*radio*
los discos compactos	*CDs*	**la videocasetera**	*VCR*
la computadora	*computer*	**el estéreo**	*stereo*
el tocador de discos compactos	*CD player*		

JEWELRY

el collar	*necklace*	**el diamante**	*diamond*
la esmeralda	*emerald*	**el oro**	*gold*
la plata	*silver*	**el brazalete**	*bracelet*
el reloj	*watch*	**el rubí**	*ruby*
el anillo	*ring*		

Nota gramatical

POSSESSIVE ADJECTIVES

Possessive adjectives express the quality of ownership or possession. The possessive adjectives used in Spanish, along with their English equivalents, are listed in the chart on the next page.

POSSESSIVE ADJECTIVES		
SINGULAR	PLURAL	ENGLISH TRANSLATION
mi	mis	*my*
tu	tus	*your (familiar)*
su	sus	*his, her, its, your (formal)*
nuestro	nuestros	*our*
nuestra	nuestras	
su	sus	*their, its, your (formal)*

✖ Spanish possessive adjectives agree in number with the nouns they modify. They are always placed before the noun.

mi pistola   *my pistol*

tus coches   *your cars*

✖ Only **nuestro** agrees both in number and gender with the noun it modifies.

nuestro nieto   *our grandson*

nuestras casas   *our houses*

✖ **Su** and **sus** can have multiple meanings. Confusion can be avoided by using the construction: [article] + [noun] + **de** + [subject pronoun].

su libro   { el libro de él
              el libro de ella
              el libro de Ud.

sus casas   { las casas de éllos
              las casas de ellas
              las casas de Uds.

Práctica

A. **La familia.** Identify each family member below and on the next page.

1. La madre de mi madre   _____

2. El hijo de mi hermano   _____

3. La madre de mi primo   _____

4. Los padres de mi madre   _____

5. La hija de mi tío   _____

B. **Identificaciones**. Identify the relatives of *Ernesto*. Remember to use a form of the verb **ser**.

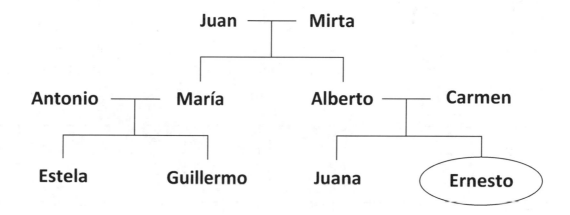

1. Juan _____.

2. Guillermo _____.

3. Antonio y María _____.

4. Estela y Guillermo _____.

5. Mirta _____.

6. Alberto y Carmen _____.

C. **Los adjetivos posesivos**. Complete each of the following sentences with the appropriate form of the possessive adjective based on the subject provided. The first one has been done for you.

1. Ella busca a **su** niño.

2. Nosotros llamamos a _____ padres.

3. Tú vas a perder _____ tren.

4. Ricardo y Ernesto quieren _____ dinero ahora.

5. Yo no encuentro _____ pistola.

6. Elena entrega _____ documentos personales al jefe.

Just for fun

Una niña perdida. You are helping Marta, a little girl who is lost in Target, to find her parents. She is telling you about them and where she lives. Unscramble the tiles to reveal what she is telling you.

C A	S	S	N A	E S T	C R	E R O	J U A	D R E
B .	R T A	E Z .	V Í C	A N	T O R	6 3	L L E	
W O O	T O	D .	L A	A P A	V	M E N	E L	
I V O	G O N	N Ú M	2 ,	P A	Z Á L	M I S	E N	
L A M	Y							

_____

_____

_____

_____

¡Así lo pronunciamos!

F, W

| f | F has the same pronunciation as the English *f* in *father*. |

FATAL   FUMAR   DIFERENTE   FÁCIL   DIFICULTAD

| w | W is only found in words borrowed from other languages and has the same pronunciation as the English letter *w*. |

WAGON   WATTAGE   WAFLE   WASHINGTON

Breaking and entering

Vocabulario útil

✖ **¿Cuándo pasó el robo?**
When did the theft occur?

✖ **¿Por dónde entraron los ladrones?**
Where did the thieves enter?

✖ **¿Qué robaron?**
What did they take?

✖ **¿Cuánto valen estas cosas?**
How much are these things worth?

✖ **¿De qué cuartos robaron?**
Which rooms did they take things from?

✖ **Vamos a necesitar una lista completa de todas las cosas que le robaron.**
We're going to need a complete list of everything they stole.

✖ **Necesitamos los color, modelo y número de serie de cada cosa, si los tiene.**
We need the color, model and serial number of each thing, if you have them.

✖ **Espere(n) aquí mientras revisamos la casa.**
Wait here while we check the house.

✖ **Vamos a buscar evidencia (pruebas).**
We are going to look for evidence.

Common stem-changing verbs

E > IE			
comenzar	*to begin*	**perder**	*to loose*
empezar		**preferir**	*to prefer*
entender	*to understand*	**querer**	*to want*
pensar	*to think*	**mentir**	*to lie*

O > UE				
almorzar	*to have lunch*	**mostrar**	*to show*
dormir	*to sleep*	**poder**	*to be able to*
encontrar	*to find*	**recordar**	*to remember*

E > I				
conseguir	*to obtain*	**repetir**	*to repeat*
pedir	*to ask for*	**seguir**	*to follow*
perseguir	*to pursue*	**servir**	*to serve*

Verbs and expressions of obligation

These verbs and expressions in the chart below will come in handy when you are telling someone what they have to do or when you are giving advice. Each of the verbs and expressions below will be followed by an infinitive.

VERBS		EXPRESSIONS	
deber	*should; ought to*	**es necesario**	*it's necessary*
necesitar	*to need to*	**hay que**	*one must, has to*
tener que	*to have to*		

Un poco de todo 3

1. Cultural Diversity

Not all Hispanics are similar. They are characterized by a rich diversity as a result of their ancestors or their country of origin. Many people mistakingly use the word *Spanish* to refer to a Spanish-speaking person, regardless of their country of origin. Actually, the adjective *Spanish* is used only to designate a person or thing from Spain.

The influence of various ethnic groups in many different combinations is clearly visible throughout the Hispanic world. In Spain, for example, there are many people of with blond hair and blue eyes, as well as dark-haired Spaniards of Arabic or Roman descent.

In Latin America this ethnic mix is even more diverse. While in some regions the European influence is dominant (i.e., Chile and Argentina), in many other areas the indigenous element has combined with the European (i.e., Bolivia and Peru). And in much of the Caribbean a third element that enriches the ethnic diversity is the African heritage. Therefore, a Hispanic can be black, white, or brown-skinned, with black, brown, blond, or even red hair, and have brown, blue, green, or even hazel eyes.

THINK ABOUT IT

What images come to mind when you think about Hispanics?

1. Things that you associate with Hispanics.

   _____

2. Cultural aspects of the Hispanic world that you think are different from the non-Hispanic world.

   _____

3. Cultural aspects that you think are similar.

   _____

2. El presente progresivo

To form the present progressive tense in Spanish, the present tense of **estar** is used with **the present participle**. To form the present participle for **–ar** verbs, drop the infinitive ending and add **–ando**. To form the present participle for **–er** and **–ir** verbs, drop the infinitive ending and add **–iendo**.

		HABLAR	COMER	SALIR
yo	estoy	habl**ando**	com**iendo**	sal**iendo**
tú	estás	habl**ando**	com**iendo**	sal**iendo**
él ella Ud.	está	habl**ando**	com**iendo**	sal**iendo**
nosotros	estamos	habl**ando**	com**iendo**	sal**iendo**
ellos ellas Uds.	están	habl**ando**	com**iendo**	sal**iendo**

✖ The present progressive tense shows that the action of the verb is in the process of taking place. Contrary to English, the Spanish present progressive is not used to refer to actions that take place over a long period of time or an action that will take place in the future.

Los prisoneros **están limpiando** las celdas.

The prisoners are cleaning the cells.

El agente **está traduciendo** el documento.

The agent is translating the document.

✖ The present participle of **–ir** stem-changing verbs also have a stem change in the present participle

sentir **sintiendo** medir **midiendo** dormir **durmiendo**

✖ An unaccented **i** between two vowels becomes the letter **y**.

creer   **creyendo**   oír   **oyendo**   distribuir   **distribuyendo**

✖ The present participle of the verb **ir** is irregular (**yendo**) and is rarely used in spoken Spanish.

A. Give the correct form of the present participle for each verb below.

   1. decir   _____

   2. pintar   _____

   3. leer   _____

   4. vender   _____

   5. distribuir _____

   6. escribir   _____

   7. pedir   _____

   8. nadar   _____

   9. aprender _____

 10. morir   _____

B. Rewrite each of the following sentences using the present progressive.

   1. Los prisioneros vacían los bolsillos.

     _____.

   2. Miguel separa los pies.

     _____.

3. Yo saco dinero del banco.

    _____.

4. El capitán cachea al sospechoso.

    _____.

5. El policía y el acusado entran en la cárcel.

    _____.

6. Nosotros ponemos el dinero en un sobre.

    _____.

7. Tú llamas al juez.

    _____.

8. Mi esposa consigue una licencia de conducir.

    _____.

9. Ud. obedece las reglas.

    _____.

10. La madre busca a su niña.

    _____.

3. Un repaso de vocabulario

C. **Rompecabezas**. Complete the crossword puzzle on the next page by writing the answers to the clues below. Page numbers have been included to help you find the clues.

ACROSS

2.   El padre de mi madre. **97**

4.   Nosotros ponemos la . . . cuando queremos ver *Friends*. **98**

6.   ¿Quiere una orden de . . . ? **81**

8.   Necesito mandar una carta. ¿Dónde está la oficina de . . . ? **88**

11.   Preparas la comida en la . . . **98**

12.   Tú **ESTAR** equivocado. La corte está en la calle Bolívar. **88**

15.   Necesito un . . . para cortar los vegetales. **74**

16.   ¿Cuál de ustedes . . . ? **80**

17.   Ud. tiene el . . . de guardar silencio. **72**

18.   Sara pone su carro en el . . . cuando llega a casa. **98**

19.   Los niños **SER** cubanos. **43**

DOWN

1.   Mi madre está mal. Está en el . . . **88**

3.   Yo voy al . . . para depositar dinero. **88**

5.   703 **57**

7.   ¡Salga con las . . . arriba! **73**

9.   7th **57**

10.   200 **57**

13.   ¿Hay armas de . . . adentro? **81**

14.   Yo no **CONDUCIR** rápido. **A-5**

16.   Es contra . . . **81**

4. Un repaso de los verbos

D. **Rompecabezas.** Complete the crossword puzzle on the next page by writing the present tense of each verb form. Review pages **50 – 51, 74 – 76** and **90 – 91** before beginning this activity. Look on pages **A2 – A6** in the appendix. *The clues for the puzzle can be found on the next page.*

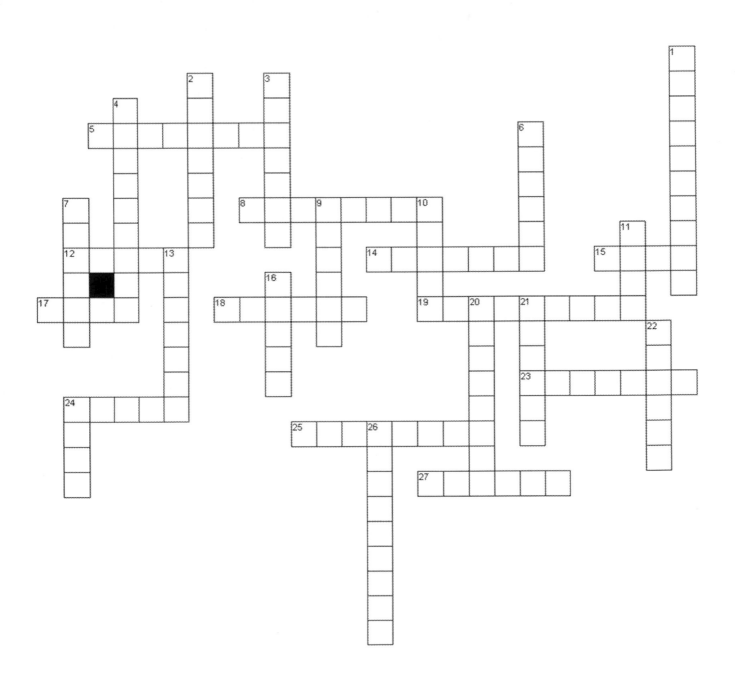

ACROSS

5. ella (devolver)

8. nosotros (pensar)

12. yo (poner)

14. yo (corregir)

15. yo (oír)

17. yo (hacer)

18. ellos (jugar)

19. yo (encontrar)

23. tú (repetir)

24. yo (salir)

25. ellos (competir)

27. yo (traer)

DOWN

1. nosotros (recordar)

2. ellos (contar)

3. ellos (mentir)

4. yo (restringir)

6. yo (perder)

7. tú (espiar)

9. ellos (situar)

10. ella (servir)

11. yo (pedir)

13. yo (ofrecer)

16. yo (tener)

20. Ud. (comenzar)

21. yo (ejercer)

22. tú (poder)

24. yo (seguir)

26. tú (preferir)

5. Dando direcciones

E. **Las preposiciones.** Complete the sentences by filling in the blank with the appropriate Spanish preposition or phrase of location.

1. Tu móvil está _____ mi ropa. **on top of**

2. Alicia vive _____ mi hermano. **close to**

3. El banco está _____ el estadio y el correo. **between**

4. Doble _____. **to the left**

5. El perro está _____ la mesa. **beneath**

6. La tienda queda _____ tu casa. **behind**

Introduction

The purpose of this chapter is to help you to be able to identify the major types of drugs, both legal and illegal, in Spanish. Vocabulary for high risk and D.W.I. traffic stops and victim / witness interrogation will also be introduced.

In This Chapter

COMUNICACIÓN

- ☑ Drug terminology
- ☑ The effects of drugs
- ☑ Traffic Stop – High Risk
- ☑ Traffic Stop – D.W.I.
- ☑ Victim / Witness Interrogation

ESTRUCTURAS

- ☑ SABER and CONOCER
- ☑ Indirect object pronouns
- ☑ Reflexive verbs
- ☑ Formal Commands
- ☑ The Preterit

1. Las drogas

The ability to understand current drug-related street terms is an invaluable tool for law enforcement, public health and other criminal justice professionals who work with the public. This list of words presented below is by no means meant to be comprehensive.

DRUGS

la coca*	} cocaine	**el crac**	} crack cocaine
la cocaine		**la roca**	
la cucaracha	roach	**el fango***	mud / brown heroin
el hachich, hachís	hashish	**la hierba, yerba***	grass
la marijuana	marijuana	**la nieve***	snow / cocaine
el polvo*	dust / cocaine	**el ácido**	acid
la anfetamina	amphetamine	**el arriba***	speed
el arriba-abajo*	upper-downer	**los barbitúricos**	barbiturates
la bombita*	booster for heroin	**el caballo***	horse / heroin
el calmante	} sedative	**los colorados**	} red devils
el sedante		**los diablos rojos***	
el crystal	ecstacy	**la heroína**	heroin
los ludis	Quaaludes	**la metadona**	methadone
la metanfetamina	methamphetamine	**la morfina**	morphine
el opio	opium	**la pastilla**	pill
el polvo de ángel	angel dust	**Ropypnol**	roofies
el sello	LSD	**el stimulante**	stimulant

* slang

THE EFFECTS OF DRUGS

el delirio	delirium	**el espasmo**	spasm
la alucinación	hallucination	**la sobredosis**	overdose

CONTINUED . . .

¡Así lo decimos!

sudar	*to sweat*	**temblar**	*to shake*
arrebatado(a)*	*stoned*	**confuso(a)***	*confused*
endrogado(a)*	*high on drugs*	**enérgico(a)***	*energetic*
hiperactivo(a)*	*hyperactive*	* these adjectives will be used with the verb ESTAR	
estar bajando	*to be coming down off a drug binge*	**estar quemado(a)**	*to be burned out on drugs*
endrogarse	*to take drugs, become addicted to drugs*	**la falta de hambre**	*lack of hunger*
la presión alta	*high blood pressure*	**las pupilas dilatadas**	*dilated pupils*
la reacción impredecible	*unpredictable reaction*	**los reflejos reducidos**	*reduced reflexes*

Nota gramatical

SABER and CONOCER

✖ Both verbs mean *to know*, but they are used differently.

SABER (TO KNOW)	
yo **sé**	nosotros sabemos
tú sabes	
él ella sabe Ud.	ellos ellas saben Uds.

SABER is used:

✖ to express knowledge of facts or information.

Yo **sé** donde están los ladrones.   *I know where the thieves are.*

Mónica no **sabe** la fecha.   *Mónica doesn't know the date.*

✖ with an infinitive. In such cases it means *to know how (to do something).*

Ricardo no **sabe manejar**.   *Richard doesn't know how to drive.*

CONOCER (TO KNOW)	
yo **conozco**	nosotros conocemos
tú conoces	
él ella conoce Ud.	ellos ellas conocen Uds.

CONOCER is used:

✖ to express familiarity or acquaintance with people, places or things. Remember to use the personal **a** when the direct object is a person.

Tú **conoces** muy bien a mi vecino.   *You know my neighbor very well.*

Conocemos la ciudad de Santiago.   *We know the city of Santiago.*

No **conozco** La Casita.   *I'm not familiar with La Casita.*

INDIRECT OBJECT PRONOUNS

An indirect object (**un complemento indirecto**), in both English and Spanish answers the question *to whom?* or *for whom?*. In English, the word **to** is often omitted. The indirect object pronouns used in Spanish are listed in the chart below.

SINGULAR		PLURAL	
me	*to, for me*	**nos**	*to, for us*
te	*to, for you*		
le	*to, for you, him, it*	**les**	*to, for you, them*

✖ The indirect object pronouns are identical to the direct object pronouns, except for the third person singular and plural forms. Because there can be some confusion with third person singular and plural, to clarify, you add a prepositional phrase. Some prepositional phrases are listed in the chart to the right.

PREPOSITIONAL PHRASES	
a él	*to him*
a ella	*to her*
a Ud.	*to you*
a ellos	*to them*
a ellas	*to them*
a Uds.	*to you all*

El policía **le** da una multa **a ella**.
   The policeman is giving her a fine.

✖ The position of indirect object pronouns follows the same rules as those of direct object pronouns. See pages **82 – 83**.

El policía **le** va a dar una multa.
El policía va a dar**le** una multa.
   The policeman is going to give him (her, you) a fine.

✖ The verb **DAR** is irregular and will require an indirect object.

DAR (TO GIVE)			
yo	**doy**	nosotros	damos
tú	das		
él		ellos	
ella	da	ellas	dan
Ud.		Uds.	

Práctica

A. **La palabra secreta.** Unscramble each of the clue words. Copy the letters in the numbered cells to other cells with the same number.

ÁDOIC   ☐☐☐☐☐
              4

RACCAAHUC   ☐☐☐☐☐☐☐☐☐
                  5

MAUNIJARA   ☐☐☐☐☐☐☐☐☐
        12   7

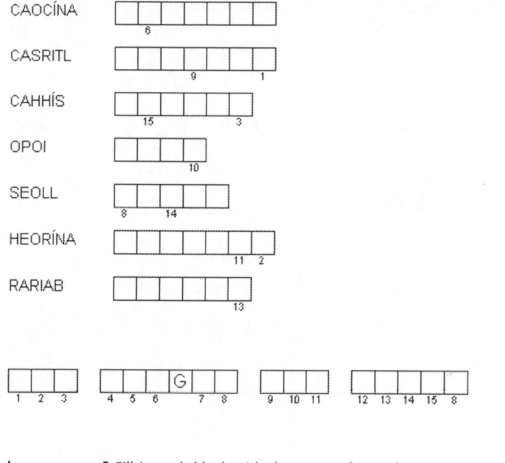

CAOCÍNA

CASRITL

CAHHÍS

OPOI

SEOLL

HEORÍNA

RARIAB

B. **¿Saber o conocer?** Fill in each blank with the correct form of SABER or CONOCER to complete the sentence.

1. Los inmigrantes no _____ hablar inglés.

2. Queremos _____ al presidente de los Estados Unidos.

3. Uds. _____ buenos hoteles en esta área.

4. Tú _____ el número de teléfono de Marta.

5. El policía _____ disparar una pistola.

6. Juan no _____ donde vivo pero _____ mi calle.

C. **Los complementos indirectos.** Complete each sentence with the appropriate indirect object pronoun. Use the cues in parentheses to help you.

1. Juan y Marta _____ van a escribir una carta desde Puerto Rico. (to me)

2. El criminal _____ da dulces. (to the children)

3. ¿Quién _____ vende la pistola? (to you, fam.)

4. Ella _____ compra ropa elegante. (for her daughter)

5. Los padres _____ muestran las drogas. (to us)

Just for fun

¿Qué vas a encontrar? You are searching a suspect's car and find an illegal substance. Unscramble the tiles below to reveal what you are going to tell the suspect.

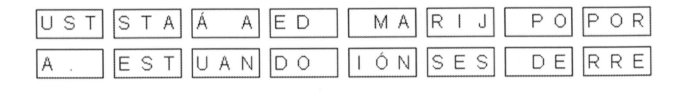

_____ .

2. Traffic Stop – High Risk

Some of your traffic stops involve dangerous encounters. Suspects are pulled over for alleged crimes and must be apprehended with as little confrontation as possible. Below are some phrases that will help you control this type of situation.

¡Chofer! / ¡Pasajero!	*Driver! / Passenger!*
¡Apague el motor!	*Turn off the engine!*
¡Tire las llaves por la ventana!	*Throw the keys out of the window!*
¡No se mueva!	*Don't move!*
¡Ponga las manos en el respaldo del asiento delantero!	*Lay your hands on the back of the front seat!*
¡Saque la mano por la ventana y abre la puerta desde afuera!	*Reach your hand out the window and open the door from the outside!*
¡Fuera del coche!	*Step out of the car!*
¡Ponga las manos arriba!	*Put your hands up!*
¡Ponga las manos detrás de la cabeza!	*Put your hands behind your head!*
¡Camine hacia mí de espalda!	*Walk backwards towards me!*
¡Arrodíllese!	*Kneel!*
¡Acuéstese boca abajo!	*Lie face down!*
¡Abre / Separe las piernas!	*Spread your legs!*

¡Así lo decimos!

Nota gramatical

REFLEXIVE VERBS

✖ A **reflexive verb** is one in which the subject is the direct receiver of the action. These verbs, when conjugated, will always have a **reflexive pronoun** that refers back to the subject of the sentence. In English this is expressed by *–self* or *–selves* (i.e., *myself, themselves*).

✖ The pronoun **se** at the end of an infinitive indicates that the verb is reflexive. When conjugated, the verb is accompanied by the reflexive pronouns listed in the chart on the next page.

SINGULAR		PLURAL	
me	*myself*	**nos**	*ourselves*
te	*yourself*		
se	*himself* *herself* *yourself*	**les**	*themselves* *yourselves*

✖ The reflexive pronoun always precedes the conjugated verb and agrees in person and number with the subject.

BAÑARSE (TO BATHE)	
yo **me** baño	nosotros **nos** bañamos
tú **te** bañas	
él ella **se** baña Ud.	ellos ellas **se** bañan Uds.

✖ Reflexive pronouns are placed after the word **no** in negative constructions.

Luisa **no** se levanta a las ocho.   *Luisa doesn't get up at 8:00.*

✖ When both a conjugated verb and an infinitive are used, the reflexive pronoun may precede the conjugated verb or attach to the end of the infinitive.

Yo **me** voy a acostar a las once.
Yo voy a acostar**me** a las once.   *I'm going to bed at 11:00.*

✖ With the present progressive, place reflexive pronouns before the conjugated form of **estar** or attach them to the present participle. When attaching a pronoun, add a written accent mark to the vowel preceding **-ndo** of the present participle.

El prisionero **se** está lavando la cara.
El prisionero está lavándo**se** la cara.   *The prisoner is washing his face.*

✖ When referring to parts of the body and articles of clothing, use definite articles rather than possessive adjectives.

Me lavo **los** dientes.   *I'm brusing my teeth.*

¿Te pones **la** bufanda ahora?   *You're putting on your scarf now?*

SOME COMMON REFLEXIVE VERBS

afeitarse	*to shave*	lavarse	*to get washed*
bañarse	*to bathe*	maquillarse	*to put on make-up*
cepillarse	*to brush*	peinarse	*to comb one's hair*
despertarse (e > ie)	*to wake up*	secarse	*to dry off*
divertirse (e > ie)	*to have fun*	vestirse (e > i)	*to get dressed*
ducharse	*to take a shower*		

VERBS WHICH CHANGE MEANING WHEN USED REFLEXIVELY

acostar (o > ue)	*to put to bed*	acostarse	*to go to bed*
casar	*to marry*	casarse	*to get married*
dormir (o > ue)	*to sleep*	dormirse	*to fall asleep*
ir	*to go*	irse	*to go away, leave*
levantar	*to raise, lift*	levantarse	*to get up*
llamar	*to call*	llamarse	*to be named*
poner	*to put, place*	ponerse	*to put on*
probar (o > ue)	*to taste*	probarse	*to try on*
quedar	*to be located, be left*	quedarse	*to stay, remain*
quitar	*to take away*	quitarse	*to take off*
sentir (e > ie)	*to feel (sorry), regret*	sentirse	*to feel*

Práctica

A. **Los verbos reflexivos.** Conjugate each verb below in the present tense.

	LLAMARSE	PONERSE	DORMIRSE
yo	_____	_____	_____
tú	_____	_____	_____
él ella Ud.	_____	_____	_____
nosotros	_____	_____	_____
ellos ellas Uds.	_____	_____	_____

B. **Más verbos reflexivos.** Rewrite each sentence with the correct present tense form of the reflexive verb in bold print.

1. Laura **lavarse** la cara y **ponerse** el sombrero.

   _____.

2. Tú **deber quitarse** la chaqueta porque hace calor.

   _____.

3. Juan y yo **quedarse** en la cama porque **sentirse** enfermos.

   _____.

4. Los prisioneros **vestirse** cada mañana a las cinco.

   _____.

5. El chico **endrogarse** después de sus clases.

   _____.

C. **¿Qué van a hacer?** Tell what each of the people below is going to do. Rewrite each sentence using the correct form of **ir + a** with the infinitive. Follow the model.

   MODELO   Roberto se baña.   *Roberto se va a bañar. / Roberto va a bañarse.*

   1. Tú te lavas el pelo.

   _____.

   _____.

   2. Yo me pruebo el uniforme.

   _____.

   _____.

   3. Mario se quita la chaqueta.

   _____.

   _____.

   4. Nosotros nos levantamos a las seis.

   _____.

   _____.

   5. Los estudiantes se duermen en la clase.

   _____.

   _____.

D. **¿Qué están haciendo?** Using the same sentences in activity C, tell what each person is doing right now. Rewrite each sentence using the present progressive. Follow the model.

   MODELO   Roberto se baña.   *Roberto se está bañando. / Roberto está bañándose.*

1. _____.

   _____.

2. _____.

   _____.

3. _____.

   _____.

4. _____.

   _____.

5. _____.

   _____.

3. Traffic Stop – D.W.I.

Being able to communicate with a drunken driver is also necessary. Below are some phrases that will help you in this situation.

Ud. estaba manejando erráticamente.	*You were driving erratically.*
¿Ha estado bebiendo alcohol?	*Have you been drinking alcohol?*
¿Ha tomado drogas?	*Have you taken drugs?*
¡Salga del coche!	*Step out of the car!*
¡Camine esta línea!	*Walk this line!*
¡Ponga un pie frente al otro!	*Put one foot in front of the other!*
¡Pare!	*Stop!*
¡Junte los pies!	*Put your feet together!*
!Extienda los brazos!	*Extend your arms!*
¡Eche la cabeza hacia atrás!	*Put your head back!*
¡Cierre los ojos!	*Close your eyes!*
¡Toque la nariz con el dedo índice derecho / izquierdo!	*Touch your nose with your right / left index finger!*
Ud. está arrestado(a) por manejar bajo el efecto del alcohol.	*You are under arrest for driving while intoxicated.*
Se le pide que se someta a una prueba química.	*You are requested to submit to a chemical test.*
Esta prueba determina el contenido de alcohol en su sangre.	*This test will determine the alcohol content of your blood.*
Si no quiere someterse a la prueba, su licencia de manejar será suspendida.	*If you refuse the test, your driving license will be suspended.*
Ud. va a tomar la prueba de <<Intoxilyzer®>>.	*You're going to take the Intoxilyzer test.*
Necesita soplar en este tubo sin parar hasta que yo le diga que pare.	*You need to blow into this tube without stopping until I tell you to stop.*
La prueba muestra que el nivel del alcohol en su sangre es más que del que se permite por la ley al operar un vehículo motor.	*The test shows that the level of alcohol in your blood is above that which is allowed by law while operating a motor vehicle.*

¡Así lo decimos!

Ud. pasó la prueba.   *You passed the test.*

Ud. tiene el derecho de irse.   *You have the right to go.*

Nota gramatical

FORMAL COMMANDS

✖ The **command** form of a verb is used to tell people what to do. To give a command, you would use the **Ud.** form for one person and the **Uds**. form for more than one person.

✖ To form the Ud. and Uds. commands of regular verbs, drop the **–o** ending from the first-person singular of the present tense and add **–e(n)** for **–ar** verbs and **–a(n)** for **–er** and **–ir** verbs.

	COMMAND FORM	
VERB	**UD.**	**UDS.**
hablar	habl**e**	habl**en**
leer	le**a**	le**an**
escribir	escrib**a**	escrib**an**

✖ Stem-changing verbs have the same stem change as in the present indicative.

	COMMAND FORM	
VERB	**UD.**	**UDS.**
cerrar	cierr**e**	cierr**en**
mostrar	muestr**e**	muestr**en**
servir	sirv**a**	sirv**an**

CONTINUED . . .

✖ Verbs that are irregular in the present tense **yo** form, maintain the irregular form in the command form. See pages **90 – 91** and **A2 – A6**.

	COMMAND FORM	
VERB	**UD.**	**UDS.**
traer	traig**a**	traig**an**
escoger	escoj**a**	escoj**an**
incluir	incluy**a**	incluy**an**

✖ Verbs ending in **–car**, **–gar** and **–zar** have spelling changes in the command form.

	COMMAND FORM	
VERB	**UD.**	**UDS.**
buscar	bus**que**	bus**quen**
pagar	pa**gue**	pa**guen**
cruzar	cru**ce**	cru**cen**

✖ The following verbs have irregular command forms.

	COMMAND FORM	
VERB	**UD.**	**UDS.**
dar	**dé**	**den**
estar	**esté**	**estén**
ir	**vaya**	**vayan**
ser	**sea**	**sean**
saber	**sepa**	**sepan**

CONTINUED . . .

✖ Place **no** before an affirmative command to make it negative.

¡**No** pegue a su esposo!   *Don't hit your husband*!

✖ Objects and reflexive pronouns must be attached to the end of affirmative commands. A written accent mark is placed over the stressed vowel of commands of more than one syllable when the object or reflexive pronoun is attached.

¡Acu**é**stese en el estómago!   *Lie on your stomach*!

¡H**á**galo ahora!   *Do it now*!

✖ Object and reflexive pronouns precede negative commands.

¡No se acueste en el estómago!   *Don't lie on your stomach*!

¡No lo haga ahora!   *Don't do it now*!

Práctica

A. **Los mandatos formales**. Write the **Ud**. and **Uds**. command forms for each verb below.

COMMAND FORM

VERB	UD.	UDS.
1. venir	_____	_____
2. pedir	_____	_____
3. dirigir	_____	_____
4. escribir	_____	_____
5. irse	_____	_____
6. buscar	_____	_____

7. abrir   _____   _____

8. ser   _____   _____

9. quitarse   _____   _____

10. cubrir   _____   _____

B. **Hablando con los niños**. You are talking to a group of students at Acosta Elementary School about personal safety and cleanliness. Tell them to do or not to do the following things.

1. Lavarse las manos antes de comer.

   _____.

2. Jugar en la calle cuando hay mucho tráfico.

   _____.

3. Ayudar a los padres con los quehaceres domésticos.

   _____.

4. Decir siempre la verdad.

   _____.

5. Cruzar la calle sin mirar.

   _____.

6. Fumar cigarillos.

   _____.

7. Recoger la ropa sucia del suelo.

   _____.

8. Volver a casa después de la medianoche.

_____.

9. Cepillarse los dientes.

_____.

10. Decir mentiras a los demás.

_____.

C. **Una motorista conduce borracha**. You have just stopped Sara Sánchez Molina for erratic driving. Tell her in Spanish to do the following.

1. Turn off the engine.

_____.

2. Show me your license and registration.

_____.

3. Get out of the car.

_____.

4. Stretch out your arms.

_____.

5. Close your eyes.

_____.

6. Touch your nose.

_____.

7. Walk the line.

_____.

8. Pick up the coins.

_____.

9. Count on your fingers.

_____.

10. Recite the alphabet.

_____.

11. You passed the test.

_____.

12. You have the right to go.

_____.

4. Victim / Witness Interrogation

This type of interrogation requires you to obtain both general as well as specific details. Use the questions below to file a report or begin an investigation.

¿Quién llamó a la policía?	*Who called the police?*
¿Quién es la víctima?	*Who is the victim?*
¿Quién vio lo que pasó?	*Who saw what happened?*
¿Cuándo pasó esto?	*When did this happen?*
Escriba su nombre, dirección y número de teléfono.	*Write your name, address and telephone number.*
El sospechoso, ¿es hombre o mujer?	*Is the suspect a man or woman?*
¿Había más de un sospechoso?	*Was there more than one suspect?*
¿Cuántos?	*How many?*
¿Conoce al sospechoso?	*Do you know the suspect?*
¿Cuál es su nombre?	*What's his / her name?*
¿De qué edad?	*How old?*
¿Cómo es la cara?	*What's his / her face like?*
¿Cómo es el sospechoso?	*What's the suspect like?*
¿De qué raza es?	*What's his / her race?*
¿De qué tamaño es?	*What size is he / she?*
¿Es joven o viejo(a)?	*Is he or she young or old?*
¿De que color son el pelo y la piel?	*What color are his / her hair and skin?*
¿Qué ropa llevaba el sospechoso?	*What clothing was the suspect wearing?*
¿Se fue el sospechoso a pie o en vehículo?	*Did the suspect leave on foot or in a vehicle?*
¿Qué tipo de vehículo?	*What type of vehicle?*
¿Vio Ud. la placa?	*Did you see the license plate?*
¿Tenía el sospechoso un arma?	*Did the suspect have a weapon?*
¿Qué tipo de arma?	*What type of weapon?*

¡Así lo decimos!

Nota gramatical

THE PRETERIT TENSE

The **preterit tense** describes an action that was completed at a definite time in the past. There are two sets of endings: one for **–ar** verbs and one for **–er** and **–ir** verbs.

	LLEVAR (TO WEAR, TAKE, CARRY)	COMPRENTDER (TO UNDERSTAND)	ABRIR (TO OPEN)
yo	llev**é**	comprend**í**	abr**í**
tú	llev**aste**	comprend**iste**	abr**iste**
él ella usted	llev**ó**	comprend**ió**	abr**ió**
nosotros (as)	llev**amos**	comprend**imos**	abr**imos**
ellos ellas ustedes	llev**aron**	comprend**ieron**	abr**ieron**

✖ Verbs ending in **–car**, **–gar** and **–zar** have a spelling change only in the **yo** form.

buscar   yo bus**qué** . . . | jugar   yo ju**gué** . . . | empezar   yo empe**cé** . . .

✖ Stem-changing **–ir** verbs in the present tense also have a stem change in the preterit, but only in the third-person singular and plural forms.

PEDIR (TO ASK FOR)		[e > i]
yo ped**í**	nosotros ped**imos**	
tú ped**iste**		
él ella **pidió** Ud.	ellos ellas **pidieron** Uds.	

CONTINUED . . .

DORMIR (TO SLEEP)		[o > u]
yo dormí	nosotros dorm**imos**	
tú dorm**iste**		
él ella **durmió** Ud.	ellos ellas **durmieron** Uds.	

✖ Verbs ending in **–er** and **–ir** and whose stems end in a vowel will take a **y** in the third-person singular and plural forms. **Leer** and **oír** also belong to this group.

INCLUIR (TO INCLUDE)		[i > y]
yo inclu**í**	nosotros inclu**imos**	
tú inclu**iste**		
él ella **incluyó** Ud.	ellos ellas **incluyeron** Uds.	

Práctica

A. **Las conjugaciones**. Conjugate each verb below in the preterit tense.

	MORIR	DISTRIBUIR	DECIDIR
yo	_____	_____	_____
tú	_____	_____	_____
él ella Ud.	_____	_____	_____
nosotros	_____	_____	_____
ellos ellas Uds.	_____	_____	_____

	PREFERIR	COMENZAR	CREER
yo	_____	_____	_____
tú	_____	_____	_____
él ella Ud.	_____	_____	_____
nosotros	_____	_____	_____
ellos ellas Uds.	_____	_____	_____

B. **El pretérito**. Rewrite each sentence, changing the verb from the present to the preterit.

1. El ladrón roba las joyas.

   _____.

2. Ellos piden un extintor.

   _____.

3. Marta llega en una ambulancia.

   _____.

4. Juan consigue controlar el coche.

   _____.

5. Los niños lloran cuando los ladrones les roban las bicicletas.

   _____.

6. Las chicas se sienten bien.

   _____.

7. La señora Jiménez sirve de intérprete.

_____.

8. Mi madre cierra la puerta de la casa con llave.

_____.

9. Enrique prefiere hablar con su abogado

_____.

10. Juan lee el periódico.

_____.

11. Pago la cuenta.

_____.

IRREGULAR PRETERITS

There are many irregular preterits and there forms must be memorized.

✘ Verbs with a **u** in the stem

	ESTAR	PODER	PONER	SABER	TENER
yo	estuve	pude	puse	supe	tuve
tú	estuviste	pudiste	pusiste	supiste	tuviste
él ella Ud.	estuvo	pudo	puso	supo	tuvo
nosotros	estuvimos	pudimos	pusimos	supimos	tuvimos
ellos ellas Uds.	estuvieron	pudieron	pusieron	supieron	tuvieron

✖ Verbs with a **i** in the stem

	HACER	**QUERER**	**VENIR**
yo	**hice**	**quise**	**vine**
tú	**hiciste**	**quisiste**	**viniste**
él ella Ud.	**hizo**	**quiso**	**vino**
nosotros	**hicimos**	**quisimos**	**vinimos**
ellos ellas Uds.	**hicieron**	**quisieron**	**vinieron**

✖ Verbs with a **j** in the stem (includes all verbs ending in **–ducir**)*

	DECIR	**TRAER**	**TRADUCIR**
yo	**dije**	**traje**	**traduje**
tú	**dijiste**	**trajiste**	**tradujiste**
él ella Ud.	**dijo**	**trajo**	**tradujo**
nosotros	**dijimos**	**trajimos**	**tradujimos**
ellos ellas Uds.	**dijeron**	**trajeron**	**tradujeron**

* Note that the 3rd person plural form ends in **–eron** instead of **–ieron**.

CONTINUED . . .

OTHER IRREGULAR VERBS

	DAR	IR	SER	VER
yo	di	fui	fui	vi
tú	diste	fuiste	fuiste	viste
él				
ella	dio	fue	fue	vio
Ud.				
nosotros	dimos	fuimos	fuimos	vimos
ellos				
ellas	dieron	fueron	fueron	vieron
Uds.				

Práctica

Rewrite each sentence, changing the verb from the present to the preterit.

1. Tú quieres sacar foto.

   _____.

2. Mis hermanos y yo venimos en coche.

   _____.

3. Uds. hacen las maletas.

   _____.

4. Paul y Eduardo van a Guatemala.

   _____.

5. Nosotros damos muchos paseos en el parque.

   _____.

6. Tienes que trabajar.

   _____.

7. Estoy en la casa de mi primo.

   _____.

8. Juan y Miguel pueden divertirse en casa.

   _____.

9. Ella no conduce muy bien.

   _____.

10. Nosotros decimos la verdad.

    _____.

USES OF THE PRETERIT TENSE

✖ The preterit is used to express an action that was completed at a definite time in the past.	Llamé a la una.
	    I called at 1:00.
	
	Él vivió en Puerto Rico por tres años.
	    He lived in Puerto Rico for 3 years.

The preterit is also used to refer to actions in the past that:
 	
✖ were performed a specific number of times.
 	
✖ were part of a series of events.
	Te llamé tres veces.
	    I called you three times.
	
	El criminal quebró la ventana, entró en la casa, y mató al perro.
	    The criminal shattered the window, entered in the house and killed the dog.

✖ The preterit is also used for sudden changes of moods, feelings or opinions.	Cuando vi a Juan, me enojé. *When I saw Juan, I got angry.*

CONTINUED . . .

✖ The preterit is frequently associated with phrases that pinpoint a particular occasion or specific time frame. If the action occurred in the past, and you can determine precisely when it occurred or how many times it occurred, then you use the preterit.

anoche
last night

ayer
yesterday

ayer por la mañana
yesterday morning

ayer por la tarde
yesterday afternoon

anteayer
the day before yesterday

desde el primer momento
from the first moment

durante tres siglos
for two centuries

el lunes por la noche
Monday night

el mes pasado
last month

el otro día
the other day

la semana pasada
last week

Drug Questions

Vocabulario útil

✖ **¿Qué está haciendo en esta área?**
  What are you doing in this area?

✖ **¿Dónde consiguió esto?**
  Where did you get that?

✖ **¿Ha estado arrestado(a) antes?**
  Have you been arrested before?

✖ **¿Cuándo comenzó a tomar drogas?**
  When did you start using drugs?

✖ **¿Tiene cicatrices o tatuajes?**
  Do you have any scars or tattoos?

✖ **¿Cuál es el nombre de su conexión?**
  What's the name of your contact?

✖ **¿Para qué es el bíper?**
  What's the beeper for?

✖ **¿Cuánto le costó?**
  How much did it cost you?

✖ **¿Cuándo lo compró?**
  When did you buy it?

✖ **¿Dónde lo compró?**
  When did you buy it?

Un poco de todo 4

1. Spanglish in the United States

Spanglish can be generally defined as any form of Spanish that employs a large number of English loanwords, especially as substitutes for existing Spanish words. It is very difficult to avoid the influence of English on the Spanish spoken in the United States. Spanish is evolving, as do all living languages. The biggest change is the infiltration of English vocabulary. You will find that many words in English are assimilated into Spanish.

> Terminación, remodelación de basement, baños, cambios de siding, ventas, puertas

2. The Imperfect Tense

The imperfect is the other simple past tense in Spanish. To form the imperfect tense in Spanish, remove the infinitive ending and add imperfect endings. There are two sets of endings: one for **–ar** verbs and one for **–er** and **–ir** verbs.

REGULAR VERBS

	HABLAR	COMER	SALIR
yo	habl**aba**	com**ía**	sal**ía**
tú	habl**abas**	com**ías**	sal**ías**
él			
ella	habl**aba**	com**ía**	sal**ía**
Ud.			
nosotros	habl**ábamos**	com**íamos**	sal**íamos**
ellos			
ellas	habl**aban**	com**ían**	sal**ían**
Uds.			

> Stem-changing verbs do not show a change in the imperfect since the imperfect is formed from the infinitive.

> Only the first person plural of **–ar** verbs has a written accent mark. All **–er** and **–ir** verbs have a written accent mark.

IRREGULAR VERBS

	IR	SER	VER
yo	iba	era	veía
tú	ibas	eras	veías
él			
ella	iba	era	veía
Ud.			
nosotros	íbamos	éramos	veíamos
ellos			
ellas	iban	eran	veían
Uds.			

> These are the only three irregular verbs in the imperfect tense.

USES OF THE IMPERFECT TENSE

The imperfect is used to refer to actions in the past that occurred:	
✖ repeatedly.	Yo visitaba a mi abuela todos los veranos. *I used to visit my grandmother every summer.*
✖ over an extended period of time.	Su familia vivía en Venezuela muchos años. *His family lived in Spain for many years.*
✖ The imperfect tense is also used to "set the stage" for an event that occurred in the past.	Yo cruzaba la calle cuando vi a Carlos. *I was crossing the street when I saw Carlos.*
	CONTINUED . . .

✖ Expresses most descriptions; mental, physical and emotional states; time and age in the past.	No sabía que estabas triste anoche. *I didn't know that you were sad.* Eduardo se sentía enfermo anoche. *Edward was feeling sick last night.* El sospechoso era alto. *The suspect was tall.* Eran las dos de la mañana. *It was 2:00 in the morning.* María tenía diez años. *María was 10 years old.*
✖ The imperfect is used with words and phrases that describe the frequency of past actions.	a menudo *often* a veces *sometimes* todos los días, cada día *every day* cada año *every year* frecuentemente, con frecuencia *frequently* de vez en cuando *from time to time* en aquella época *at that time* generalmente *generally*

CONTINUED . . .

Notes	
	muchas veces *many times*
_____	mucho *a lot*
_____	
_____	nunca *never*
_____	
_____	por un rato *for awhile*
_____	
_____	siempre *always*
_____	
_____	tantas veces *so many times*
_____	
_____	todas las semanas *every week*
_____	
_____	todo el tiempo *all the time*

A. **Las conjugaciones**. Complete the verb charts in the Appendix on page A-18.

3. Formal Commands

B. **¡Todos a bordo!** Read the security instructions for a typical airplane flight. You are not going to understand every word. Try to understand the main ideas. Write the **Uds**. command form for each verb in parentheses.

Buenos días y bienvenidos a bordo. Ahora unas medias de seguridad. (Abrocharse[1]) en cinturón de seguridad. (Mantener[2]) el respaldo del asiento en posición vertical, la mesa en la posición inicial y (poner[3]) su equipaje en de mano completamente debajo del asiento de adelante o en uno de los compartimientos de arriba. Por favor, (obedecer[4]) el aviso de no fumar. En el respaldo del asiento, delante de Uds., hay una tarjeta con información. Esta tarjeta les indica la salida de emergencia más cercana. (tomar⁵) unos minutos para leerla.

En este avión hay dos puertas en cada extremo de la cabina y dos salidas sobre las alas. En caso de que sea necesario, el cojín del asiento puede usarse como flotador: (pasar⁶) los brazos por los tirantes que están debajo del cojín. Si hay un cambio brusco de presión en la cabina, los compartimientos que contienen las mascaras de oxígeno se abren automáticamente. Entonces, (ponerse⁷) la máscara sobre la nariz y la boca y respiren normalmente. Después, (tomar⁸) la cinta elástica y (ponersela⁹) sobre la cabeza. Después de ponerse la mascara, (ajustar¹⁰) bien la mascara de sus niños. Gracias por su atención y esperamos que tengan un buen viaje.

1. _____

2. _____

3. _____

4. _____

5. _____

6. _____

7. _____

8. _____

9. _____

10. _____

APPENDIX

Verbs with spelling changes in the present tense

INTRODUCTION

This section introduces more verbs that have a spelling change in the present tense. You are not expected to memorize all of the information presented here. Review this section as many times as you need.

A BRIEF REVIEW

Conjugating verbs is very easy in Spanish. The endings for Spanish verbs are listed in the chart below.

SUBJECT	VERB TYPE		
	AR	ER	IR
yo	o	o	o
tú	as	es	es
él ella Ud.	a	e	e
nosotros	amos	emos	imos
ellos ellas Uds.	an	en	en

✖ Verbs ending in –uir

These verbs (not including those that end in –**guir**) add **y** after the **u** in all forms, except for **nosotros**.

INCLUIR (TO INCLUDE)

yo	inclu**y**o
tú	inclu**y**es
él ella usted	inclu**y**e
nosotros (as)	incluimos
ellos ellas ustedes	inclu**y**en

atribuir	*to attribute*
concluir	*to conclude*
construir	*to construct*
contrubuir	*to contribute*
destruir	*to destroy*
diminuir	*to diminish*
distribuir	*to distribute*
excluir	*to exclude*
huir	*to flee*
influir	*to influence*
obstruir	*to obstruct*
sustituir	*to substitute*

CONTINUED . . .

✖ Verbs ending in **–iar** and **–uar**

These verbs stress the **i** or the **u** (**í, ú**) in all forms except **nosotros**.

ENVIAR (TO SEND)

yo	env**í**o
tú	env**í**as
él ella usted	env**í**a
nosotros (as)	enviamos
ellos ellas ustedes	env**í**an

CONTINUAR (TO CONTINUE)

yo	contin**ú**o
tú	contin**ú**as
él ella usted	contin**ú**a
nosotros (as)	continuamos
ellos ellas ustedes	contin**ú**an

-IAR

confiar (en)	*to rely (on), confide (in)*
espiar	*to spy*
fiarse (de)	*to trust*
resfriarse	*to catch cold*
vaciar	*to empty*
variar	*to vary*

-UAR

actuar	*to act*
evaluar	*to evaluate*
graduarse	*to graduate*
situar	*to situate*

✖ Verbs ending in **–ger** and **–gir**

The **g** changes to a **j** before the **o** in order to maintain the soft sound of the infinitive. In the present tense, this change only occurs in the first-person singular (**yo** form).

ESCOGER (TO CHOOSE)

yo	**escojo**
tú	escoges
él ella usted	escoge
nosotros (as)	escogemos
ellos ellas ustedes	escogen

CONTINUED . . .

Dirigir (to direct, conduct)

yo	**dirijo**
tú	diriges
él ella usted	dirige
nosotros (as)	dirigimos
ellos ellas ustedes	dirigen

-GER

coger	to grab, catch
encoger	to shrink
proteger	to protect
recoger	to gather, pick up

-GIR

afligir	to afflict
corregir (e > i)	to correct
elegir (e > i)	to elect
fingir	to pretend
restringir	to restrict
sumergir	to submerge

✖ Verbs ending in –guir

The **gu** changes to **g** before **o** in order to maintain the hard sound of the infinitive. In the present tense, this change only occurs in the first-person singular (**yo** form).

Distinguir (to distinguish)

yo	**distingo**
tú	distingues
él ella usted	distingue
nosotros (as)	distinguimos
ellos ellas ustedes	distinguen

seguir*	to follow
conseguir*	to get, acquire
perseguir*	to persue, persecute
proseguir*	to proceed
extinguir	to extinguish

*See page 76.

✖ Verbs ending in –cer and –cir

The **c** changes to **z** before **o**. In the present tense, this change only occurs in the first-person singular (**yo** form).

Convencer (to convince)

yo	**convenzo**
tú	convences
él ella usted	convence

CONTINUED . . .

nosotros (as)	convencemos
ellos ellas ustedes	convencen

ESPARCIR (TO SCATTER)

yo	**esparzo**
tú	esparces
él ella usted	esparce
nosotros (as)	esparcimos
ellos ellas ustedes	esparcen

-CER

mecer	*to rock*
ejercer	*to exercise*
vencer	*to conquer, overcome*
cocer (o > ue)	*to cook*
torcer (o > ue)	*to twist*

✖ Verbs ending in –**ducir**

The **c** changes to **zc** before **o**. In the present tense, this change only occurs in the first-person singular (**yo** form).

TRADUCIR (TO TRANSLATE)

yo	**traduzco**
tú	traduces
él ella usted	traduce
nosotros (as)	traducimos
ellos ellas ustedes	traducen

conducir	*to drive*
deducir	*to deduce*
introducir	*to introduce*
lucir	*to shine*
producir	*to produce*
reducir	*to reduce*
reproducir	*to reproduce*

✖ Verbs ending in –**cer** and –**cir**

These verbs have a vowel before –**cer** and –**cir**. The **c** changes to **zc** before **o**. In the present tense, this change only occurs in the first-person singular (**yo** form).

CONOCER (TO KNOW)

yo	**conozco**
tú	conoces
él ella usted	conoce

CONTINUED . . .

nosotros (as)	conocemos
ellos ellas ustedes	conocen

AGRADECER (TO THANK)

yo	**agradezco**
tú	agradeces
él ella usted	agradece
nosotros (as)	agradecemos
ellos ellas ustedes	agradecen

agradecer	*to thank*
aparecer	*to appear*
crecer	*to grow*
desaparecer	*to disappear*
establecer	*to establish*
fortalecer	*to strengthen*
merecer	*to deserve*
obedecer	*to obey*
ofrecer	*to offer*
parecer	*to seem*
permanecer	*to remain*
pertenecer	*to belong*

Notes

_____

_____

_____

_____

_____

_____

_____

_____

_____

_____

_____

_____

_____

_____

_____

_____

_____

_____

_____

_____

_____

_____

_____

Present Tense - Verb Review

A. Regular **-ar**, verbs

	YO	TÚ	ÉL, ELLA, UD.	NOSOTROS	ELLOS, ELLAS, UDS.
amar					
bailar					
sacar					
tomar					
gastar					
visitar					
regresar					
mirar					
trabajar					

B. Regular **-er** and **-ir** verbs

	YO	TÚ	ÉL, ELLA, UD.	NOSOTROS	ELLOS, ELLAS, UDS.
comprender					
aprender					

	YO	TÚ	ÉL, ELLA, UD.	NOSOTROS	ELLOS, ELLAS, UDS.
escribir					
comer					
permitir					
vender					
decidir					
consistir					
prometer					
leer					
creer					
recibir					

C. Stem-changing verbs **e → ie**

	YO	TÚ	ÉL, ELLA, UD.	NOSOTROS	ELLOS, ELLAS, UDS.
preferir					
empezar					
comenzar					
pensar					
querer					

	YO	TÚ	ÉL, ELLA, UD.	NOSOTROS	ELLOS, ELLAS, UDS.
entender					
perder					
mentir					
negar					

D. Stem-changing verbs **o → ue**

	YO	TÚ	ÉL, ELLA, UD.	NOSOTROS	ELLOS, ELLAS, UDS.
recordar					
volver					
dormir					
almorzar					
encontrar					
mostrar					
poder					
contar					
soñar					
costar					
devolver					

	YO	TÚ	ÉL, ELLA, UD.	NOSOTROS	ELLOS, ELLAS, UDS.
morir					

E. Stem-changing verbs **e → i**

	YO	TÚ	ÉL, ELLA, UD.	NOSOTROS	ELLOS, ELLAS, UDS.
pedir					
repetir					
servir					
seguir					
corregir					
elegir					
competir					
impedir					

F. Stem-changing verb **u → ue**

	YO	TÚ	ÉL, ELLA, UD.	NOSOTROS	ELLOS, ELLAS, UDS.
jugar					

G. Verbs irregular in the **yo** form

	YO	TÚ	ÉL, ELLA, UD.	NOSOTROS	ELLOS, ELLAS, UDS.
hacer					
traer					
poner					
salir					
dar					
saber					
ver					
producir					
traducir					
conocer					
agradecer					
crecer					
merecer					
obedecer					
ofrecer					

H. Irregular verbs

	YO	TÚ	ÉL, ELLA, UD.	NOSOTROS	ELLOS, ELLAS, UDS.
ser					
estar					
ir					
tener					
venir					
oír					
decir					

I. Reflexive verbs

	YO	TÚ	ÉL, ELLA, UD.	NOSOTROS	ELLOS, ELLAS, UDS.
despertarse					
ponerse					
bañarse					
sentarse					
acostarse					

	YO	TÚ	ÉL, ELLA, UD.	NOSOTROS	ELLOS, ELLAS, UDS.
quedarse					
dormirse					
irse					

Preterit Tense - Verb Review

A. Regular **-ar**, **-er** and **-ir** verbs

	YO	TÚ	ÉL, ELLA, UD.	NOSOTROS	ELLOS, ELLAS, UDS.
amar					
vivir					
comprender					
pensar					
vender					
consistir					
perder					
cerrar					
decidir					

B. Verbs irregular in the yo form [**-car**, **-gar** and **-zar** verbs]

	YO	TÚ	ÉL, ELLA, UD.	NOSOTROS	ELLOS, ELLAS, UDS.
buscar					
pagar					

	YO	TÚ	ÉL, ELLA, UD.	NOSOTROS	ELLOS, ELLAS, UDS.
comenzar					

C. Verbs with a **y** in the 3rd person singular and plural forms

	YO	TÚ	ÉL, ELLA, UD.	NOSOTROS	ELLOS, ELLAS, UDS.
leer					
oír					
caer					
construir					
contribuir					
destruir					
creer					
poseer					

D. Stem-changing verbs **e → i, o → u**

	YO	TÚ	ÉL, ELLA, UD.	NOSOTROS	ELLOS, ELLAS, UDS.
pedir					

Preterit Tense - Verb Review

	YO	TÚ	ÉL, ELLA, UD.	NOSOTROS	ELLOS, ELLAS, UDS.
preferir					
servir					
dormir					
conseguir					
competir					
morir					
corregir					
elegir					
repetir					
mentir					

E. Irregular preterits

	YO	TÚ	ÉL, ELLA, UD.	NOSOTROS	ELLOS, ELLAS, UDS.
estar					
poder					
poner					
saber					

	YO	TÚ	ÉL, ELLA, UD.	NOSOTROS	ELLOS, ELLAS, UDS.
tener					
hacer					
querer					
venir					
decir					
traer					
traducir					
dar					
ir					
ser					
ver					

Imperfect Tense - Verb Review

A. Regular verbs

	YO	TÚ	ÉL, ELLA, UD.	NOSOTROS	ELLOS, ELLAS, UDS.
amar					
vivir					
comprender					
pensar					
dormir					
pedir					
jugar					
levantarse					

B. Irregular verbs

	YO	TÚ	ÉL, ELLA, UD.	NOSOTROS	ELLOS, ELLAS, UDS.
ser					
ir					
ver					

Vocabulary Log

SPANISH WORD	ENGLISH EQUIVALENT

SPANISH WORD	ENGLISH EQUIVALENT

SPANISH WORD	ENGLISH EQUIVALENT

SPANISH WORD	ENGLISH EQUIVALENT